digital 3d design

SIMON DANAHER

SERIES CONSULTANT
ALASTAIR CAMPBELL

**WATSON-GUPTILL
PUBLICATIONS**
New York

First published in the
United States in 2001 by
Watson-Guptill
Publications, a division of
BPI Communications, Inc.,
770 Broadway, New York,
NY 10003

This book was conceived,
designed, and produced by
The Ilex Press Limited
The Barn, College Farm
1 West End, Whittlesford
Cambridge CB2 4LX

Sales Office
The Old Candlemakers
West Street, Lewes
East Sussex BN7 2NZ

Publisher:
Sophie Collins
Art Director:
Alastair Campbell
Editorial Director:
Steve Luck
Design Manager:
Tony Seddon
Project Editor:
Caroline Earle
Designers:
Jane and Chris Lanaway

ISBN 0-8230-1296-4

Library of Congress
Control Number:
2001092957

Originated and printed
by Hong Kong Graphics
and Printing Ltd., China

WORKING IN THREE DIMENSIONS

3D computer graphics are everywhere—in the latest blockbuster movie, TV advertisements, the Web, and in magazines. In fact, there is barely any form of visual communication that has not been transformed or improved by digital technology, and 3D graphics lie at the core of the revolution. If you enjoy problem solving, creativity, and rewarding yet hard work, then you will enjoy working in 3D computer graphics and animation.

What this book aims to do is break down the elements of the 3D thought process and try to explain what 3D is all about—the techniques, the jargon, and the tools. This does not necessarily mean that the book is only for beginners. Established 3D artists will gain something from it too. Understanding what 3D is all about and exploring its inner workings are essential if you are to progress through the early stages to become a 3D digital guru.

If you come from a 2D paint, image editing, layout, or Web design background, or have just never used a 3D program before, the world of 3D modeling and animation may seem daunting. Rather than the two dimensions of a flat canvas, your canvas is now space itself, a volume that you have to fill with light, texture, color, and movement.

Actually the design disciplines that apply to 2D work also apply to 3D; it's just the working methods and tools that change. Form, color, composition, and texture are equally important in 3D design as they are in more traditional design practices, and why wouldn't they be?

1
The 3D landscape generator Bryce has often been the weapon used to assault our senses. The world doesn't need any more images of crusty terrains and infinite oceans under candy-colored skies.

2
If you really want to see what not to do, it's worth taking a trip to the Gallerie Abominate at **www.jackals-forge.com**. This particular specimen is a prime example of just how bad it can get.

the GALLER
ABOMINA

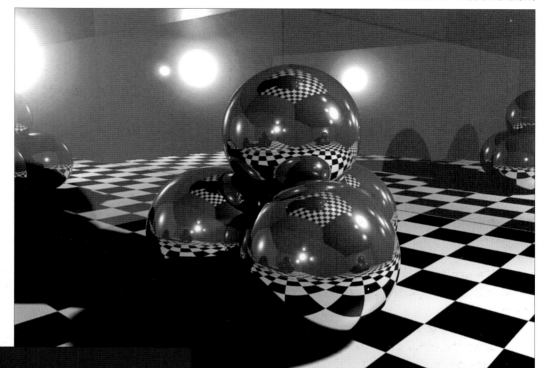

3
First experiments with raytracing often look like this image of perfectly reflective chrome balls in a reflective room. A good test for rendering speed, but that's about it.

MOSS ISLEY GOES MENTAL

The upshot of this is that if you are a good designer you will be a good 3D designer. No amount of technique will make up for little talent or lack of aptitude for design. Unfortunately, most 3D design work we see, especially that which adorns countless Web sites across the globe, is often created by the latter category of artist. Bad design is bad design, no matter how you dress it up.

Because most 3D programs, especially the inexpensive ones, make it easy for novices to create "spectacular" imagery with very little effort or time, this is often the kind of 3D work that people see most frequently. Fantasy landscapes with neon skies and crystal-clear waters, chrome balls, hard shiny objects, and flying logos made of shimmering gold are just some of the regular examples of quick and easy design. We've all seen them and probably made them at some point, but these types of images don't do justice to what is really possible with 3D digital art.

8

LEARNING TO SEE

Just as a traditional fine artist learns to see rather than merely look, so must the 3D artist. Simple things, such as the properties of everyday materials or the subtleties of human movement and expression, become fascinating subjects of study and examination for the dedicated 3D artist. Every day you will see something new, something that can be added to your understanding of the way things appear or behave.

A direct comparison can be made between the way fine art developed in the last two millennia and the current developments and studies that are occurring in the realm of 3D computer graphics.

Early in the history of painting, perspective was poorly understood and even more poorly reproduced. It wasn't long, however, before artists were able to accurately simulate 3D spatial and perspectival effects, at least sufficiently to create the illusion of depth and space that could fool the eye, even if it was not 100 percent accurate.

The Presentation of the Virgin (1305) by Giotto shows how early in the history of art perspective was not always well represented.

Leonardo da Vinci's painting of *The Last Supper*, (1498) in the Convent of Santa Maria delle Grazie, in Milan was used to great effect to simulate an extension of the room in which it was painted. The painting shows a table at which the disciples and Jesus are feasting, but the room in which they are sitting extends backward with exaggerated perspective, which, though not exactly accurate, works as a visual illusion.

An even greater achievement was made by Michelangelo with his painting of the Sistine Chapel ceiling. An incredibly complex and impressive work, this elevated fresco also demonstrates incredibly subtle 3D touches. What appear at first to be detailed structures in the architecture of the chapel ceiling are, on closer inspection, the work of Michelangelo's hand.

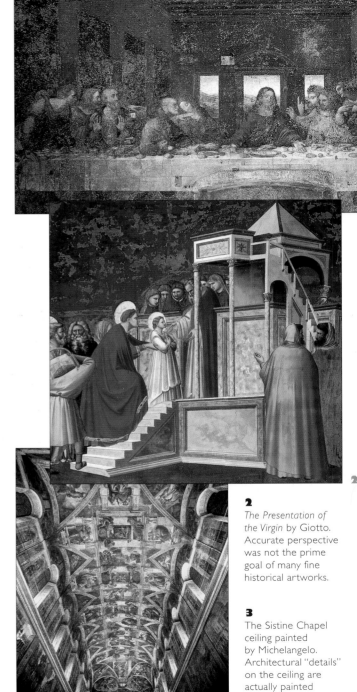

2
The Presentation of the Virgin by Giotto. Accurate perspective was not the prime goal of many fine historical artworks.

3
The Sistine Chapel ceiling painted by Michelangelo. Architectural "details" on the ceiling are actually painted by the artist.

1

The Last Supper by Leonardo da Vinci. The fresco is situated in an elevated position on the end wall. The exaggerated perspective makes it seem as though the feast is happening in an adjoining room.

The understanding and rendering of the effects of light by later painters, such as Van Eyck, Canaletto, and Vermeer, are incredible. Vermeer, in particular, painted simple pictures where the event or subject depicted was of secondary importance. Composition, light, and form were the prime focuses in these seminal works of art.

What has this brief departure into the history of painting got to do with 3D graphics, I hear you ask? The accurate description of the effects of light is of just as much importance to the 3D artist seeking realism as it was to the painters described above. A good 3D artist is able to push his or her tools to the limit in order to produce beautifully lit and rendered 3D scenes. A push-button solution to the production of credible computer imagery does not yet exist. Thankfully, we have talented 3D artists instead.

4 | 5

These two paintings, *The Art of Painting* and *Young Woman with a Water Jug* by Vermeer, both demonstrate wonderful attention to detail with respect to the light in the scenes.

NEW TECHNIQUES

One of the great advances made in the world of computer imagery has been accomplished by Paul Debevec at the University of Southern California's Institute for Creative Technologies. Debevec's approach to creating truly realistic rendering is to accurately capture the huge dynamic range that is experienced first by the human eye.

Photography produces believable imagery by its very design. It records an image of the real world using a lens system similar to that of the human eye, and with similar limitations and artifacts (such as glare, blur, etc.). Where the photographic system falls down is in capturing and reproducing the dynamic range that the eye experiences.

Dynamic range is the measure of the range of brightness values that a given system can record. The human eye can detect massive variations in brightness values, for example. We don't need to change our retinas for more sensitive ones in low-light conditions, as our eyes and brains can adapt (though this may take a few seconds or minutes in extremely low light). However, the film in a camera can't always cope with such a wide range of intensities.

1 | 2 | 3
By accurately capturing the light in a real environment (in this case St. Peter's Basilica, Rome) using variable-level, multiple-exposure photography, an image can be created to "light" a 3D scene reproducing that environment. These images are created using the high-dynamic-range imagery lighting technique by Paul Debevec. His film *Fiat Lux* depicts these dark monoliths falling like dominoes inside St. Peter's Basilica. The monoliths are 3D models—as is the backdrop of St. Peter's, except that it has been created using photos of the real building. The lighting illuminating the 3D scene is from St. Peter's too, so it all looks very natural.

2

3

What Debevec's research has shown is that, by using multiple photographs of an environment that have employed a wide range of different exposure levels, it is possible to capture an image with a much wider dynamic range. The sequence of photos is scanned into a computer and the brightness values gathered into a single image that contains the entire dynamic range captured across the multiple exposures.

While a computer display cannot present this image in a greater range of brightnesses than its monitor can display, the image can be used for different purposes, such as lighting a 3D scene. By recording an environment using this high-dynamic-range technique, it can then be used in a 3D program that supports this special image format to accurately recreate the lighting of the original environment. Not only the intensity but the color and direction of the light are recreated. The end result is arguably the most realistic computer imagery that has ever been produced. You can sample some of Paul Debevec's work at **www.debevec.org.**

13

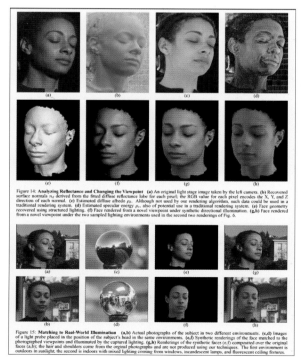

Figure 14: **Analyzing Reflectance and Changing the Viewpoint** (a) An original light stage image taken by the left camera. (b) Recovered surface normals n_d derived from the fitted diffuse reflectance lobe for each pixel; the RGB value for each pixel encodes the X, Y, and Z direction of each normal. (c) Estimated diffuse albedo ρ_d. Although not used by our rendering algorithm, such data could be used in a traditional rendering system. (d) Estimated specular energy ρ_s, also of potential use in a traditional rendering system. (e) Face geometry recovered using structured lighting. (f) Face rendered from a novel viewpoint under synthetic directional illumination. (g,h) Face rendered from a novel viewpoint under the two sampled lighting environments used in the second two renderings of Fig. 6.

Figure 15: **Matching to Real-World Illumination** (a,b) Actual photographs of the subject in two different environments. (c,d) Images of a light probe placed in the position of the subject's head in the same environments. (e,f) Synthetic renderings of the face matched to the photographed viewpoints and illuminated by the captured lighting. (g,h) Renderings of the synthetic faces (e,f) composited over the original faces (a,b); the hair and shoulders come from the original photographs and are not produced using our techniques. The first environment is outdoors in sunlight; the second is indoors with mixed lighting coming from windows, incandescent lamps, and fluorescent ceiling fixtures.

4
Another project by Paul Debevec involves capturing the "reflectance field" of a human face. The images you see here are from a computer model of an actress, which is being rendered using different high-dynamic-range image environments.

4

SOFTWARE

The most important tool a 3D artist has (aside from a desire to create, and his or her own inventiveness and skill) is 3D software. What follows is a brief compendium of some of the most popular 3D programs that are available today.

Maya

Maya was developed by Alias|Wavefront as the 3D application to end all 3D applications, at least as far as character animation and effects are concerned. It is considered by many to be the holy grail of 3D animation, and because of its sheer power and flexibility it has become a firm favorite throughout the 3D graphics industry. From film effects to product visualization, fine art, and games, Maya is fast becoming the standard by which all others are judged.

Maya's core operating strategy is based on nodes. Everything in Maya is a node with an input and an output, so that you can connect various nodes together to create custom events and effects. Maya also features powerful technology, including built-in dynamics simulation, fur and cloth simulation, and an impressive set of modeling tools.

Maya is available on SGI IRIX, Windows NT/2000, Linux, and Mac OS X.

14

2

1

Maya is the de facto standard in high-end 3D animation. Like Photoshop it has become the program by which all others are judged.

1

Photorealistic RenderMan

Photorealistic RenderMan is the rendering program created and used by Pixar to make the fantastic images we've seen in movies such as *Toy Story* and *Jurassic Park*. It has become a rendering standard used in the film industry because of its exceptional quality. Because of its wide acceptance, many other programs can link to it, effectively replacing their built-in rendering engines.

Based on a technology called REYES (Renders Everything You Ever Saw), Photorealistic RenderMan, or PRMan, as it is known for short, fulfilled the two main criteria required for 3D graphics to be used effectively for film production. First, it was fast; and second, it could simulate the motion-blurring effect of a motion picture camera, thus making it possible to integrate 3D-rendered imagery with live-action footage.

PRMan is available for Windows NT, SGI IRIX, Sun SPARC, and Linux.

15

2
Though Maya was used for plenty of the effects and animation in the film *The Mummy*, much of the rendering was done with Pixar's Photorealistic RenderMan software.

3
A classic image from Photorealistic RenderMan. Though the PRMan standard supports all kinds of rendering methods, PRMan does not use raytracing *(see pages 88–89)*. Many raytracing effects, such as reflections, can be easily "faked."

4
Photorealistic RenderMan creates images using the REYES rendering algorithm (Renders Everything You Ever Saw) and supports high-quality displacement mapping.

Softimage 3D and Softimage XSI

Softimage 3D was one of the first 3D animation packages designed with artists in mind. Before its release, most 3D software was proprietary and developed by enthusiasts, researchers, or professionals working in the film industry. Most of the software required a degree in programing or mathematics to use it, so it was difficult for traditional 3D stop-motion animators to operate. Softimage 3D provided ease of use, so that talented animators could be put to work creating digital 3D animation.

Many of the characters that you see in films are still created using Softimage 3D, though in recent times Maya has slowly taken over in this department. Softimage has recently released their next-generation 3D product, XSI, which incorporates many new and advanced features, including Mental Image's Mental Ray rendering engine.

Softimage is available for use on SGI IRIX, Windows NT, and Linux.

Lightwave 3D

Lightwave 3D is actually made up of two programs—Modeler, which handles the building and texturing of 3D objects, and Layout, which allows you to animate and render them. It has become a popular choice for 3D artists working in film, broadcasting, and games because of its high-quality rendering and comprehensive toolset.

2
XSI uses Mental Ray for its rendering. Mental Ray is a very high-quality renderer and capable of stunning results.

The Pick of the Month is the ultra-photorealistic work of Ulf Lundgren, a Modeler and Texture Artist working with Filmtecknarna in Sweden.

1
This old man was created in XSI and is a prime example of just how good the results from the program can be.

16

Originally developed on the Amiga platform, Lightwave 3D was designed to provide 3D effects for video production. It has since blossomed into a fully fledged 3D animation system that is capable of advanced modeling and animation with excellent rendering quality.

Lightwave was one of the first commercial packages to provide subdivision surface modeling in the form of MetaNURBS technology (*see pages 56–57*). Though the concept of Subdivision Surfaces had been around for a while, Lightwave's MetaNURBS let artists build organic-looking single-skin models with relative ease. Similar systems are now available in most popular 3D programs.

One of the main reasons for the program's popularity is that, from the outset, the program has had an extendable architecture, meaning that third-party developers can write plug-ins that extend Lightwave's functionality. There is also a large number of free and shareware plug-ins available, so an artist can easily expand the toolset without having to part with a great deal of extra money.

Lightwave is currently available for Windows, IRIX, Sun Solaris, and Macintosh computers, including OS X.

4
Lightwave 3D is used in film, broadcast, games, and multimedia. Rendering quality is very high and the program features excellent organic modeling in the form of MetaNURBS *(see pages 56–57).*

3
Lightwave has been a popular choice for producing 3D animations and effects for SciFi TV series, including *Babylon 5* and *Star Trek: The Next Generation.*

Cinema 4D XL

Like Lightwave, Cinema 4D began life on the Amiga, before migrating to the PC and Macintosh platforms. The current version, dubbed XL, features impressive modeling and animation tools coupled with one of the fastest raytrace rendering engines available. XL is one of the few programs at its price point that has relational modeling capabilities in the form of a proprietary hierarchical modeling system. Subdivision Surfaces are supported, and there are also tools for character animation.

Maxon produces new versions of the software at a fast rate, rivaling Alias and Maya in this respect. In the fast-paced world of 3D technology this is a feature not to be underestimated: because technology becomes rapidly outdated. Cinema 4D is also expandable via plug-ins—there are not quite as many available as for Lightwave, but many are free. The latest version features a new antialiasing system, fast radiosity, and caustics rendering, and workflow tools such as multipass rendering output.

Cinema 4D XL is available for use on Macintosh and Windows PCs.

3
Cinema 4D XL has a modeling system that features a hierarchical pipeline that helps to keep the modeling process "live" and accessible.

2
Like Lightwave, Cinema 4D XL is well suited to broadcast work, character design, and print graphics. The program is also very fast at rendering.

1
Cinema 4D XL has become increasingly popular thanks to the fast development pace provided by its developers, Maxon. Maxon was also one of the first companies to express its commitment to develop for Mac OS X.

18

4
ElectricImage is particularly good at rendering very large scenes containing millions of polygons. The rendering is very high quality and fast.

5
The latest version of ElectricImage (called ElectricImage Universe) has much better support for complex areas of 3D animation.

5

4

19

ElectricImage

Used on films such as *Terminator 2* and *Star Wars Episode I: the Phantom Menace*, ElectricImage one of the best 3D animation systems. Not only does ElectricImage have exceptional quality rendering that can rival PRMan, it is also the fastest renderer around today. Until recently, the program was limited to rendering and animation. If you wanted to model you had to use another 3D program—usually AutoDesSys's Form•Z, at the time an animationless modeling and rendering program. ElectricImage now comes with its own separate modeling program, based on Spatial Technology's ACIS geometry kernel, and offers a high-precision solid- and surface-modeling environment. The very latest version of ElectricImage, dubbed EI Universe, adds raytracing (*see pages 88–89*) to its rendering capabilities, and additional modeling features. Subdivision surface modeling is on offer, too, in the form of UberNURBS, a similar system to Lightwave's MetaNURBS system.

ElectricImage is available for Macintosh, Windows PCs, and Sun Solaris workstations.

3D Studio Max

3D Studio Max is one of the most popular 3D programs.
Discreet, the developer, would have us believe that it is
the best-selling 3D animation package, though this may
not be the whole truth. The company has an aggressive
education licensing policy and Max is the program that
many budding 3D artists learn on in education
establishments. It's often believed, usually by newcomers
to 3D, that Max is the be all and end all of 3D graphics,
but, while it is competent, this is certainly not the case.

Max was a development of 3D Studio, the DOS
program that had become a popular choice for 3D
animation on the desktop. It was completely rewritten
for Windows NT to take advantage of the more
advanced operating system. Recently, Discreet has
tempered criticism of its rendering quality by making
Mental Ray available as a plug-in renderer at extra cost.
Like Lightwave, Max is buoyed by a large third-party
developer community and can boast a vast number of
free and shareware plug-ins.

3D Studio Max is available for Windows NT and 2000.

mental images

"WALKING WITH DINOSAU[...]
Directed by Tim Haines
© BBC SCIENCE / DISCOV[...]
Computer Animation and Sp[...]
Visual Effects by FrameStor[...]
Images rendered with menta[...]

1 | 2
Mental Ray is a high-
quality rendering
system and competes
with RenderMan in the
high-end world of 3D
rendering. Supporting
technology such as
radiosity and caustics,
it has been used in
many films, notably
Fight Club.

3
Max has a modular
design and the basic
package has Inverse
Kinematics (IK) and
character tools. For
advanced characters
you will need the
Character Studio plug-in.

4
3D Studio Max has
long been a favorite
for game production,
but recently it has
lost ground to
competing packages.

Sony goes on a WildTangent
with **3ds max** for *A Knight's Tale*

4

3

5
Lightscape is dedicated to radiosity rendering. Radiosity calculates the indirect illumination in a scene and is capable of stunning realism.

Mental Ray

Mental Ray is a raytrace renderer made by Mental Images GmbH. This program features a sophisticated shading language and has been used most famously in tandem with Softimage 3D and XSI.

Mental Ray is an application that features exceptionally high rendering quality and supports a vast array of effects, such as the simulation of natural light phenomena through radiosity and caustics.

Mental Ray is available to use with 3D programs running on Windows PCs and Silicon Graphics IRIX workstations.

Lightscape

Lightscape is another rendering application, but one that focuses primarily on radiosity. This application is often used by companies creating architectural visualizations because of the extremely accurate way it handles the subtleties of lighting. This is important because it allows architects to get an accurate picture of the way a building reacts to real lighting conditions. Simulations can be performed for both artificial and natural lighting, and sun studies can be performed that will indicate how the spaces in the building will look at different times of the year.

Lightscape is available for use on Windows PCs.

6
Lightscape has no modeling tools of its own. You must model elsewhere and import the scene for texturing, lighting, and final rendering.

2

5

Rendered using the Lightscape Visualization System

21

POVray

POVray (Persistence Of Vision RAYTRACER) is a rendering application that generates raytraced rendering of the scenes with which you supply it. It's a command line renderer, so it has no graphical user interface as such, and is therefore popular with pros as well as enthusiasts and hobbyists.

POVray is available for MS DOS, Windows 95/NT, Macintosh, Linux, Sun OS, Unix, and Amiga.

TrueSpace

TrueSpace is another 3D program with a long history. Recently, the company that developed the program, Caligari, has introduced novel features that take advantage of the powerful graphics capabilities in today's desktop computers. The entire interface can be displayed as a 3D scene, with tools and features rendered using OpenGL or Direct 3D in real time.

The program features animation and modeling tools, as well as raytrace rendering, complete with hybrid radiosity.

TrueSpace is available for Windows PCs.

Rhino

Robert McNeel and Associates' Rhino is an industrial-strength 3D-modeling program that harnesses the power and flexibility of NURBS modeling to great effect. The Rhino 3D-modeling program is mainly a modeling program with basic rendering for visualizing the objects that you create, though there are indications that a high-quality rendering engine will be included in later versions.

Rhino is available for use on Windows PCs.

1
POVray is a popular freeware-rendering program that supports raytrace and radiosity rendering and is available on most platforms.

2
TrueSpace is a mid-range 3D animation program that has a good set of features including NURBS modeling and radiosity rendering. Image quality is high considering the price.

22

Bryce

Bryce whipped up a storm of enthusiasm when it was first introduced, and it still has legions of devoted users. It's primarily a landscape and environment generator that can be used to create all sorts of realistic and fantasy scenarios with the bare minimum of user input. Should you want to get deeper into the creation of Bryce images, it offers more sophisticated tools, too.

Bryce was a groundbreaking 3D program in many ways, not least because of its love-it-or-loathe-it interface, which has candy buttons and hidden features. Based on a raytracing renderer, Bryce allows you to create simple animations and high-resolution stills. The modeling is not as comprehensive as it is in other 3D applications because it was never intended to be an all-around 3D program. Most of the modeling in Bryce can be done using primitive objects and Boolean rendering, though the Terrain Editor is a tool that allows you to sculpt landscapes using a simple grayscale-to-height mapping scheme.

Bryce is available for use on both Macintosh and Windows PCs.

3

4

Bryce is a landscape generator that can be used to create all manner of 3D worlds. You can also create basic objects and import 3D models.

Bryce tends to be a "one-click art" type of program. The rendering quality is average but it is capable of very good output with some effort.

3

Rhino is an industrial-strength NURBS modeling system with basic rendering, decent OpenGL support, and comprehensive tools.

23

Poser

From the same stable as
Bryce, Poser broke similar
new ground as the first
commercial 3D program
that could be used to
create procedural human
figures. Poser people are
now ubiquitous in 3D
graphics and are highly
recognizable, but the
program has numerous
high-quality features, such
as a procedural walk
generator, motion output
(so that you can create
animations in Poser and
apply them to different models in another 3D
program), lip synching, and animation.

You can also import "props," other 3D objects
created elsewhere, which Poser figures will hold,
wear, or interact with.

Original developer MetaCreations (now
Viewpoint) sold Poser when it shed its graphics
division to concentrate on Web 3D development, but
thankfully it was bought by a company comprising
the original MetaCreations development team. Called
Curious Labs, the company is continuing the
development of this popular 3D program.

Poser is available for use on Macintosh and
Windows PCs.

1

1
Poser is a dedicated
figure-designing
system. It can be used
to create 3D human
characters using a
library of preset
humans, which can be
modified extensively.
It can be used for
animation, too, and
features IK (*see page
136*) and a good
timeline. Rendering
quality is average, but
images can be easily
touched up.

2
Strata has a very
good raytrace
renderer, which, in
the Pro version,
includes radiosity.

2

24

3

There are three versions of Strata 3D: a free version called *base*, a paid-for version with extra features called *plus*, and the full, paid-for version, *pro*.

Strata 3D

An old favorite, Strata 3D features a good selection of tools for what is now a relatively low-end product, at least in terms of price. The *base* version is available free of charge, while extra features are available in the paid for version, *plus*.

The full version, *pro*, features raytracing and radiosity rendering, as well as animation and effects. Strata 3D is available for Windows and Macintosh.

Pixels 3D

Based on NURBS modeling, Pixels 3D is an accomplished 3D system for the Macintosh. It features a workstation-like interface that is reminiscent of high-end offerings, such as the original Softimage 3D. It also has a good raytrace renderer.

Interestingly, the company is currently developing a rendering system called Tempest, a program which is closely based on Pixar's PRMan and can be used to render across networks with great versatility.

Pixels 3D is available for the Macintosh only.

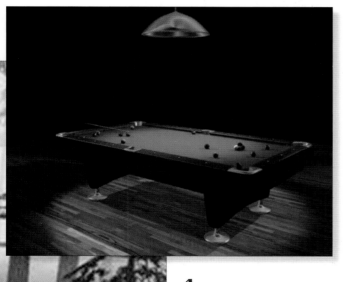

4

Pixels 3D is a Mac-only 3D animation program. It's based on NURBS and has a lot of very powerful features, yet it is affordable. The animation tools in Pixels are very good. There are IK, some clever, render-based NURBS-blending features, scripting and other high-end tools.

25

Hash Inc.—Martin Hash Animation Master

Hash Animation Master is a deeply satisfying animation program to use. Not only does it make 3D character animation relatively straightforward, but it also does so for very little money—about as much money as a decent Max plug-in, in fact.

Its IK and joints system are fantastically designed and put many more expensive 3D programs to shame. The geometry is based on proprietary Hash Patches, well suited to character animation work.

Animation Master is available for Macintosh and Windows PCs.

1

Animation Master is well thought-out and is exceptional in some areas (notably character animation).

ElectricImage Inc.—Amorphium

Amorphium is ElectricImage's other 3D package. It is based on a 3D-sculpting theme, so you can take simple primitive objects and mold them like putty into almost any shape that you want. It does this using OpenGL display and a hoard of tools, ranging from displacing brushes to deforming modifiers (bend, twist, bulge, etc.).

The program also offers radiosity rendering and raytracing and has Flash output for a quick and painless way to get pseudo-3D animations onto the Web.

Amorphium is available for Macintosh and Windows PCs.

Avalanche Software

2

Amorphium allows you to mold and sculpt objects, then texture and render them using radiosity.

3

Using Amorphium you can push, pull, twirl, and twist basic forms into any shape you can imagine.

26

4
ImageModeler can be used to create 3D models from photographs.

5

5
ImageModeler requires little setup or information about the camera system used, and can literally recreate any kind of shape.

6

3

6
ImageModeler is particularly useful for creating 3D objects for the Web, but is also used for feature films and effects work.

RealVIZ—ImageModeler

Developed by RealVIZ, ImageModeler is one of the most intriguing 3D products that has come along in recent times. Rather than working from scratch, building up a model of a 3D object using polygons or NURBS, a lot of special tools, and even more patience, RealVIZ suggests that you should use a photograph. It sounds too good to be true, or even possible, yet this is exactly what ImageModeler achieves.

By taking a series of photographs of the object to be modeled from different angles, together with a reference target, ImageModeler can reconstruct the object in 3D to a high degree of accuracy.

The user simply marks out the same points on the target (a simple grid of points)—which is of a known shape—in each photograph and ImageModeler uses this as a calibration guide. You then do exactly the same for the object, marking the details in each picture. Eventually, when enough samples have been taken, the software does some nifty calculations and builds a polygon mesh that does indeed represent the object. The software also extracts textures from the photograph and applies them to the model.

The advantages of the RealVIZ Image Modeler are obvious, since almost any shape object can be reconstructed. However, the downside of it is that the object must exist in the first place. It does, of course, allow unique 3D models that are made out of clay to be "digitized" using this photographic technique.

ImageModeler is available for use on Windows PCs and Mac OS X.

Kaydara—FilmBox

FilmBox has captured a bit of a niche because it is one of the few 3D systems that is solely geared toward real-time animation and motion capture. Motion capture is a technique whereby an actor's movements are recorded in three dimensions as they perform. This captured motion can then be applied using some sophisticated digital rigging to animate a full 3D character.

FilmBox features impressive tools for managing complex animations, merging captured data with keyframe animation, and reducing motion capture data to a manageable number of keyframes.

FilmBox is available for Windows PCs and Mac OS X.

1 | 2
FilmBox is a motion-capture and keyframe animation program used for real-time broadcasting (e.g. virtual TV presenters and actors) and for managing motion-capture data and applying it to 3D models.

2

SolidThinking

A robust NURBS modeler and high-quality raytrace renderer, SolidThinking features polygon and subdivision surface modeling, construction history, and special analytic tools useful for product visualization and CAD. Rendering is supplied by a high-quality raytracer and there is also radiosity. SolidThinking can be used as a front end to BMRT and Photorealistic Renderman.

SolidThinking is available for Windows and Macintosh.

4
SolidThinking is a NURBS modeler that also features good polygons and subdivision surfaces tools. Rendering is good and the program can link to BMRT and Photorealistic RenderMan.

28

1

3
This image was created using BMRT, a shareware rendering program created by Larry Gritz at Pixar. The program features raytracing and radiosity and has been used in many motion pictures.

29

Blue Moon Rendering Tools

BMRT, or Blue Moon Rendering Tools, is the work of Larry Gritz, who is currently working at the world-famous Pixar animation studios. BMRT is a Renderman-compliant command line renderer that boasts complete compatibility with Pixar's Renderman RIB interface, which is the standard for the communication of scene files from modeling applications to renderers.

Unlike Photorealistic Renderman, BMRT features raytracing and radiosity and has been used to render elements in Pixar features in situations where accurate reflections precluded the use of PRMan (notably in Pixar's motion picture *A Bug's Life*). It is also a shareware product and can be used for a very small sum.

BMRT is available for Windows, Linux, SGI IRIX, and Sun Solaris.

3D COMPUTER GRAPHICS I

W̶e live in four dimensions—three spatial
dimensions and one temporal dimension. With
stereoscopic vision we can perceive depth and distance,
and our brain is also capable of discerning minute
differences in shade, texture, and movement. This
makes replicating the real world a bit tricky and
explains why 3D graphics can be very frustrating but,
thankfully, highly rewarding too. In this chapter, I hope
to introduce, as gently as possible, some of the core
concepts in 3D graphics, as well as to provide a brief
overview of the key technologies that are involved
when creating 3D imagery on a computer.

   It could be argued that 3D graphics are mainly used
to reproduce the real world for the entertainment
industry, but that's just a portion of its many and varied
uses. 3D graphics can just as easily be found being used
to create totally unreal images, and is also used in
medical research and diagnostics, training, and
visualization. The important thing to remember is that
3D graphics programs produce 2D images, regardless of
how these images are put to use. It doesn't matter how

32

2
A new 3D image
display box at an
unveiling in Tokyo. This
is the world's first 3D
image display visible
to the naked eye.

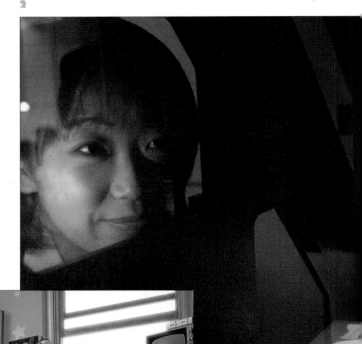

1
3D graphics as used in
the movie *Toy Story 2*.
Produced by Pixar and
Disney. *Toy Story* was
the first full-length,
completely 3D
animated movie
ever produced.

3

3
This is how we perceive the world visually, by means of 2D images projected onto our retinas. It is only because we have two forward-pointing eyes that we can perceive depth and three-dimensionality in the real world.

4

the images are presented to a viewer, be they prerendered and read back in a movie file on a computer or printed onto celluloid and projected on the big screen: the end result is just a two-dimensional image. Likewise with interactive 3D applications such as computer games, Web 3D, or virtual reality systems, the output is still a two-dimensional image, albeit blitzed to the screen in real time rather than saved on a disk.

4
On the "holo deck" in *Star Trek: The Next Generation*—the background is a hologram.

3D COMPUTER GRAPHICS 2

Stereoscopic virtual-reality systems that simultaneously display a pair of 2D images to each eye individually fool the brain into thinking it's seeing 3D, but this is still far from the real thing. There are no holographic display systems commercially available, though there is undoubtedly someone working on the problem at the time of writing. To be fair, the 3D world we live in is itself an illusion because the three-dimensionality we experience is due to our brain interpreting two slightly different 2D images projected onto our retinas.

In the world of CAD and industrial design, 3D computer programs can be used to create actual 3D objects, and this is about the only way that 3D objects can be created directly by a computer. By sending the 3D description of an object to a computerized lathe, drill, or, even better, stereolithography machine, the digital data is then converted into a real, functioning 3D object. With stereolithography a laser penetrates a vat full of a photopolymer, a special chemical substance that solidifies when struck by light of a particular wavelength and intensity (for example, by a laser). Using the digital 3D data, the laser is able to trace the volume of the object in the vat to recreate the 3D form. Unfortunately, the output is limited by the laws of physics—laws that are routinely broken in the world of 3D graphics.

34

1
Stereolithography output creates real objects by guiding laser light through a vat of a special photosensitive polymer, which solidifies when laser light of the right type and intensity strikes it. By guiding the laser beams through the vat, a 3D object is formed.

2

2
The end result of a stereolithography session is removed from the machine once the unsolidified photopolymer has been drained away.

3
A variety of objects can be created. This rapid prototyping is very useful in the world of engineering and product design, since a prototype 3D model can be created in a fraction of the time it would take a machine to make it.

ANATOMY OF 3D SPACE

3D space is the computer software's internal representation of three-dimensional space, and is a very close approximation of the space we live in. By defining three directions—x, y, and z—perpendicular to each other, we can plot the location of any point in this artificial 3D space using a measurement along each of the three directions. This space is also known as Cartesian coordinate space and was named after the French philosopher and mathematician René Descartes. Don't worry, though, you don't need to be a math whizz to understand or use Cartesian coordinates.

Where the three axes meet is the center of the computer's 3D space, which is also known as the origin. In Cartesian coordinates this has x, y, and z values of 0 and is written 0,0,0. Therefore, if you wanted to plot a point 2 units in y, 3 units in x, and 1 in z, this would be written as 2,3,1 in Cartesian coordinates.

A difficulty arises when transposing ideas into a synthetic 3D space, because a 3D artist interacts with the software on a computer using a 2D device, either a mouse or stylus, and the feedback on the computer screen is also in 2D. Somewhere in between, existing

1
The three directions x, y, and z are all that is required to define 3D space on a computer. Traditionally, these three axes are also colored for ease of identification: x is red, y is green, and z is blue, and this is true for the majority of 3D programs. There may be one or two shareware applications that don't adhere to this convention, but all the major programs do.

2 | 3 | 4
Cyber gloves (2) let you interact with 3D graphic images as if they were real. These sorts of 3D systems haven't made any real impact on our lives, but Hollywood got plenty of mileage from the concept in movies such as *The Lawnmower Man* (3, 4).

only in computer code, does the digital 3D world really exist. This can pose a problem, because it's just as easy to point your cursor at the front of an object as at its back using these 2D devices—the computer has no way of knowing which side you're interested in without some clever calculating by the software and some concentration by the artist.

This problem can be one of the most disconcerting aspects of 3D graphics, especially for beginners. There are many ways in which this particular barrier has been overcome by software companies and artists over the years. For example, cyber gloves and 3D goggles or two-handed input devices can be used. However, after a short time, a good 3D artist adapts and learns techniques that enable him or her to interact transparently with the software, without the need to use these sophisticated gadgets.

3

4

VIEWS INTO THE 3D WORLD

The 3D world that you work in on your computer can be displayed in a variety of ways. The most obvious is a single 3D view, which displays a floor grid and x, y, and z axes so that you can orient yourself in the virtual world. A virtual camera displays the view, complete with perspective, so that you can easily navigate the scene and get a feel for the 3D space. Moving the 3D view is very important because the subsequent parallax effects provide the brain with visual cues so that it can figure out where objects are in the scene. Near objects will move across the screen more rapidly than distant objects, thus exposing their true location. You can observe the parallax effect if you hold up one finger at arm's length and the other about a foot away from your nose and line them up. As you move your head from side to side the near finger will appear to move from left to right with respect to the distant finger.

Another type of view is the orthogonal view. This is a parallel 2D view, very similar to a plan of a building, and it is usually perpendicular to one of the three Cartesian axes. There are six orthogonal views, and these are often named top, left, front, back, right, and bottom. Objects that are the same shape and size appear identical in an orthogonal view, no matter how far away from each other they are. Orthogonal views are therefore useful to align objects. The other useful thing about them is that they allow you to move objects

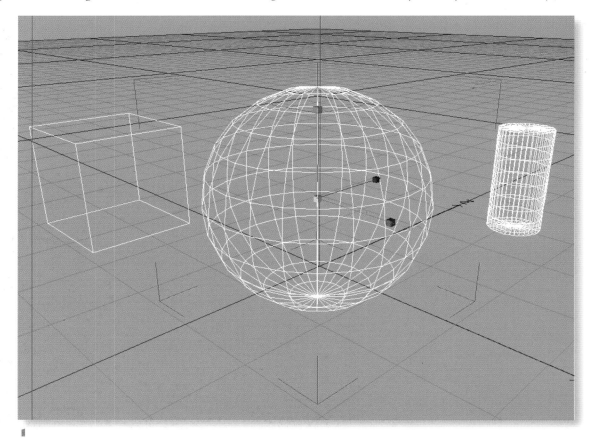

1
From this view it's not clear exactly how big the sphere is, or where it is in relation to the other two objects.

that are constrained to the view plane. You can do this in the perspective view, too, but you would have to tell the software that you wanted to move the object in x and z but not y, which would take a few extra mouse clicks. It's far easier to just drag the object in the Top view (since this is perpendicular to the xy plane).

Please note that throughout this book we will assume y to represent the Up axis of the 3D world. (Some 3D programs use y as the Up axis, while others take z to be Up.)

39

2
Moving the view discloses that the sphere is, in fact, large and distant in the scene. You'll find that as you are working on complex models, rotating the view constantly as you examine the object will give you a much better idea of its form.

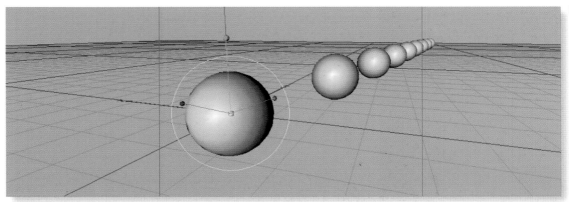

3 | 4
Similar objects viewed in an orthogonal view appear the same size regardless of their location in 3D space.

JOINING THE DOTS

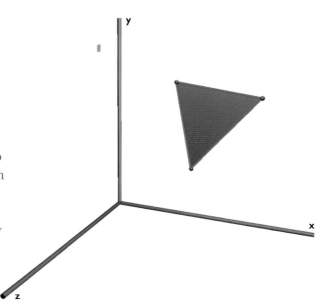

Once we have 3D space we can build 3D objects, but how do 3D programs create objects? What are they constructed from? As we've seen previously, any point in space can be defined using a set of three coordinates. Imagine these three points all lying in the same plane (but not overlapping), and imagine drawing a line from one to the next, then to the next and back to complete a triangle. If we tell the computer to fill in such a triangle, we have the simplest building block in 3D graphics, the three-point polygon. The triangle is the simplest 3D structure that can be filled in or rendered by 3D software so that it looks solid. Actually, a triangle could be thought of as a 2D object since it cannot be bent or twisted into a third spatial dimension. Triangles, therefore, have a special place in 3D graphics.

40

1
Three points that lie in the same plane (xy) are joined together with edges to make a triangle. The enclosed area is filled in to form a face that can be rendered.

2
Now, add three more triangles and join them together so they are enclosing a volume, but let them share the points and edges where they meet. This forms the simplest 3D volume—the tetrahedron. Polygons can have any number of sides and points, and any number of them can be joined together to make a 3D object.

3

A sphere can be made by joining a net of three- and four-point polygons, while other volumes such as a cylinder might have end polygons (called caps) that contain many points. Making 3D objects from polygons is called Polygon Modeling, and it's the simplest and most direct way to create 3D objects. A 3D object is defined by the points that make it up, whose locations in 3D space are precisely known by their coordinates.

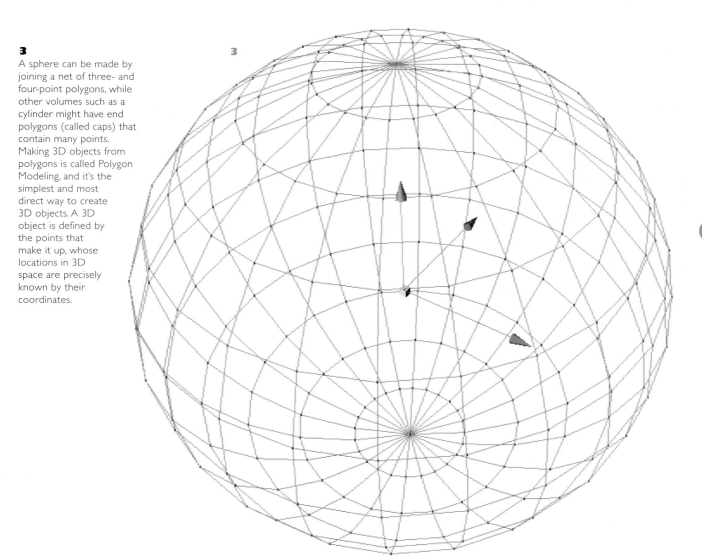

Polygons are made up of three components: points, edges, and faces. These three components represent increasing levels of complexity in the structure of 3D objects. The point is the fundamental component in 3D graphics, simply defined by its three Cartesian coordinates. It is then followed in complexity by an edge, which joins two points. This is then followed by a face, which is enclosed by three or more edges.

There is another component, which is not directly editable but is nevertheless very important, called the Surface Normal. The Surface Normal is a line that runs perpendicularly from every polygon face, though by default it is set to be invisible. Normals tell the 3D program which way the face is pointing, either toward the camera or away from it; this has important implications for shading, as we shall see later on.

TRANSFORMATION

In the world of 3D, we can select and move an object to another location, just like in the real world. We don't want our sphere here, we want it there, so we move it. It is possible to do exactly the same in a 3D application—select an object and drag it on screen in the 3D or orthogonal view to another location. Another way in which to move an object, however, is to enter precise coordinate values. Almost all 3D programs allow you to see and edit an object's coordinates, so if you know that an object is 100mm high but that it's 50mm below the ground plane—i.e. its y coordinate reads –50mm—you can simply type 0mm in order to

bring it flush with ground level. A 3D object, though, has volume. By definition it is spread about in 3D space, so from what part of a 3D object does the computer measure distances and locations? Well, all 3D objects have a local center, which is very much like the world center (the origin). In some programs, this local center is called its Local axis or the object's Pivot Point. If the object is a sphere, for example, the Pivot Point is most likely to be bang smack at the center of the sphere. Therefore, if you enter a value for the object's y coordinate, you are really entering a value for its Local axis. It is as if the object's entire

42

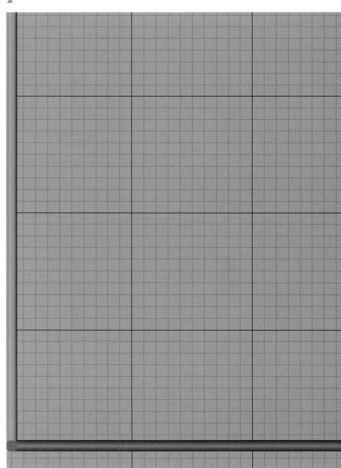

1|2
Local axes provide you with better options when it comes to transforming (moving, scaling, or rotating) objects, since an object can be transformed relative to the World coordinate system or to its own Local axis system. When both systems are aligned there is no difference between moving an object using local coordinates and moving it using World coordinates.

3
If an object is rotated on its Local z axis by about 35°, so that it is no longer in alignment with the World axis, moving the object using its (now rotated) Local x axis gives a different result from moving the object using the World x axis.

43

4

4
Mixing transformations in both coordinate systems can have odd results. Imagine two identical cubes. One is aligned with the World axes while the other is rotated around its Local z axis. Scaling both cubes in World space in only the y axis produces a different result on each cube. The aligned cube is scaled along its y axis as expected, but the rotated one has become distorted as the World y axis no longer lines up with its Local y axis. However, it will be obvious when to use Local or World coordinates.

world is being moved, because its points stay in the same location relative to the Local axis.

The great thing about using Local axes is that no matter how rotated an object is relative to the World axes, you always know which way represents its local top, front, and side direction points, and, therefore, you are easily able to move or scale it in these directions. Usually a 3D program can switch transformations (moving, scaling, and rotation) between Local and World coordinates.

MODELING

As we have seen, the polygon is the simplest building block in 3D modeling. 3D programs let you build objects point by point if you wish, although to build a complex object, such as a DC-10 airplane, point by point would take rather a long time. Point editing is also known as low-level editing because it involves editing the model at its most elementary level. What 3D programs do, however, is provide you with a layer of tools that lets you model in much broader fashion. These tools make the task of creating 3D objects much quicker and easier. But before looking at some of these in closer detail I should mention Primitive objects.

Primitives are very useful because they provide you with a set of objects that can be combined to make other objects. For example, a table can be made from five cylinders—four that have been scaled so that they are long and thin (the legs) and the other so that it is short and wide (the tabletop). In fact, if you look at real objects around you, you'll see that many of them can be broken down into a collection of various Primitives.

44

2

1

3

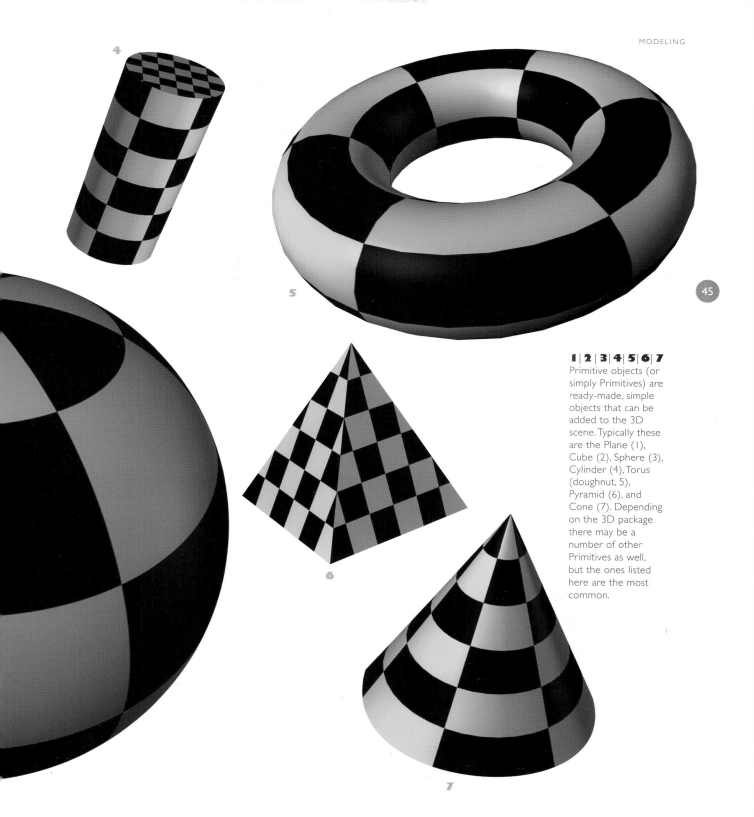

45

1|2|3|4|5|6|7
Primitive objects (or simply Primitives) are ready-made, simple objects that can be added to the 3D scene. Typically these are the Plane (1), Cube (2), Sphere (3), Cylinder (4), Torus (doughnut, 5), Pyramid (6), and Cone (7). Depending on the 3D package there may be a number of other Primitives as well, but the ones listed here are the most common.

HIGH-LEVEL TOOLS

When primitive modeling does not suffice, you will need to turn to the more hands-on polygon tools. These tools can be used on simple polygon shapes to create much more complex forms. They usually take the form of an action or operation that is performed on the simple object to create a complex one. The most straightforward of these is Extruding. Take a planar polygon (its points all lie on the same plane so it's not twisted) and literally extrude it perpendicularly and you will get a 3D volume whose cross section is the original polygon shape.

It is also possible to extrude selected polygons that are part of another 3D object. This provides you with a way to extend polygon objects quickly and easily. The direction and the amount of extrusion can be defined either by dragging in the view ports or by entering values. Here's where the Surface Normal can be extremely useful, because in many 3D applications you can use it to define the direction of the extrusion.

1
A planar polygon shape has been extruded in one direction to give it volume. Extruding is the simplest high-level polygon tool available in most 3D programs. The yellow line pointing away from the extruded polygon is its Surface Normal.

2
Any polygons can be selected and extruded, even if they are part of an object. Here two faces are selected and extruded to extend the object and add detail.

3
Lathing rotates
a profile polygon
around an axis,
building the surface
in steps as it goes. It's
like a series of small
joining extrusions,
each one rotated
slightly more than
the previous one.

Lathing is another common polygon tool. A lathe operation rotates your polygon profile around an axis in order to create the 3D form. Lathed objects are rotationally symmetrical, although you can specify the starting and ending angle of a lathe to create a partially revolved object as well. Typical objects that can be created by lathing include wine bottles, axles, vases, wine glasses, and car tires—basically anything that is rotationally symmetrical.

Lofting is a further tool for creating 3D objects from a profile, or rather a series of profiles. First you create two or more polygon profiles, then position them as if they were the cross sections of the 3D form that you want to construct. The Loft tool then connects the profiles to create an outer "skin" of polygons, which is why this tool is sometimes called the Skin tool. Lofting can be very useful for creating more organically shaped objects, although it can be difficult to visualize in advance the shapes that you need for the profiles.

4
Four sequentially rotated polygons are lofted together to form an undulating shape. Lofting can be tricky using polygons, as you can see the object is quite angular; adding more cross sections would produce a better result but take a lot longer.

CURVES, SPLINES, AND RESOLUTION

There are more polygon tools, but it is important to introduce another geometry type before we take a look at what these other tools have to offer. So far, we've seen that points in 3D space can be connected together by edges to form polygon faces, which in turn are used to build 3D models. Points can also be connected to create a curve. Curves are special objects in 3D programs because they don't render in the final image; however, it is still possible to use them as construction aids in modeling.

❚
Three points are used to create a curve instead of a polygon. Curves are defined using mathematical equations resulting in smooth flowing lines, but they only need a few points in order to be plotted.

Unlike polygonal objects, which in their simplest form are nothing more than vast collections of coordinates, curves use elegant mathematical equations to define their form. If you take three points, like those used in our triangle example earlier, but tell the computer to generate a curve rather than a polygon, you will get something very different. Unlike polygon edges, which are, by definition, linear, curves are, well, curved.

The most important property of curves is their economy. Imagine recreating a curve line using points and edges, and you'll see that it would take many more points than the three used to define the curve. A lot of extra points will mean there are a greater number of coordinates that the computer has to remember at one time. Such extra data means that the object has taken up more of the computer's resources and slowed things down.

2

If curves can't be seen in the final image, then what use are they? Well, curves can be used as paths for polygon modeling operations, such as Sweeping, whereby a polygon profile is swept along a curve to form a twisting shape. And their mathematical nature means they are also quite flexible. By using different types of equations, curves can have straight segments between points that are either made to pass through the points or not, to produce different types of curves.

Curves are often called splines—a shipbuilding-industry term. A spline, which is a thin strip of wood or metal, was used to mark out the shape of a ship's hull. Weights would be placed along the spline that would bend the spline in predictable ways. By moving the weights, the shape of the curve could easily be changed. These physical splines were the basis of the mathematical splines that we use today in 3D programs.

3

Here are four curves. All use the same arrangement of six points but are, nevertheless, different types of curve. From the top left, moving clockwise there are linear, cubic, akima, and B-spline curves. There are other types too, including Bézier and NURBS.

49

2

Sweeping is a modeling operation that uses a curve as a path along which a polygon profile is swept. Sweeping can be used to create pipes, tubes, helixes, and other twisting shapes.

3

RESOLUTION

The problem with polygons is that to make a smooth surface you need to use a lot of them—in fact hundreds or even thousands of them. And an object that has thousands of points not only takes up valuable system resources but is difficult to work with. Selecting and editing points, edges, and faces then becomes a nightmare because there are so many of them and they all can be edited to the same degree. With a goal of having fewer editable points, a different approach, called spline patching, was developed to get over the problem of how to create smooth surfaces efficiently.

50

1|2|3
In these three images you can see that as the number of polygons used in the sphere increases, so does the quality of the shaded surface. This is an important issue, since in order to have a smooth surface you need lots of polygons, but this in fact makes the object difficult to work with.

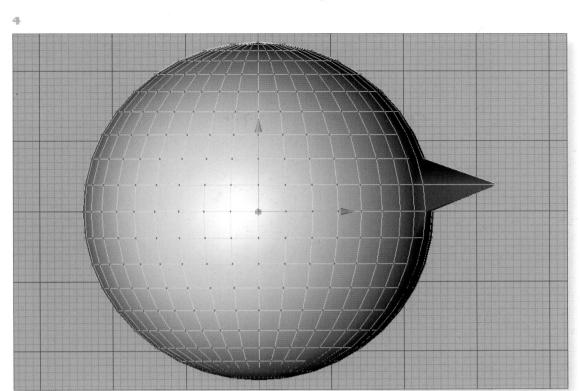

4
If you edit the points on the sphere it is very difficult to maintain the surface smoothness.

5
Better polygon tools have been developed in order to help with the problem, such as this Magnet tool. It provides a falloff effect to the area selected to help smooth the point editing into the surrounded surface, but it can still be difficult to use.

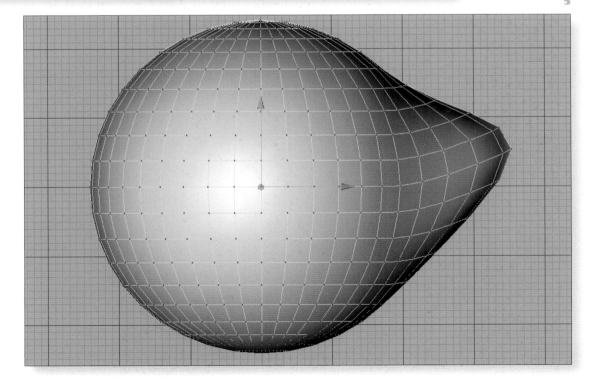

SPLINE PATCHES

Technology has now been developed that allows you to construct smooth surfaces on polygons. Rather than a web of connected polygons, a net of interconnected splines can be used instead, with the benefit that only a few points are needed to control the shape of the surface.

You can still use tools such as Extrude, Lathe, and Loft, but the profiles and paths will be made with spline curves instead of polygons. Some systems also allow you to mix the two, letting you sweep a polygon profile along a spline path, for example (Lightwave is one such program). However, you can't loft using a mixture of polygons and curves.

2

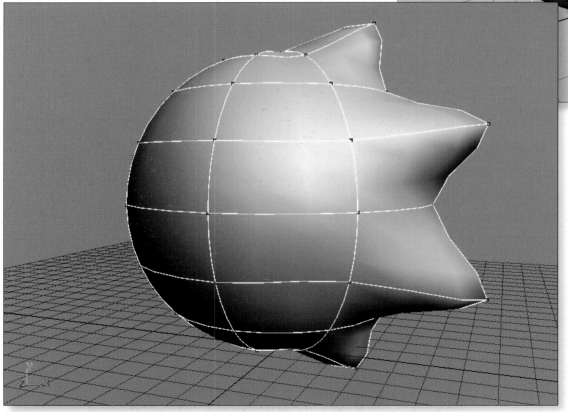

1

A surface made from a net of spline curves requires only a handful of points to achieve a smooth surface. What's more, editing the surface is much easier because there are fewer points to select and move, and the surface's natural tendency to flow from one point to the next keeps things looking smooth and organic during editing.

In order to create a surface, a grid of splines makes a network of "patches," each of which is supported by surrounding curve points. This is why spline modeling is also known as spline patching or patch modeling.

With patch modeling you can create much smoother surfaces with fewer control points than is possible with mere polygons. In the same way as for polygons, you can also connect splines in more or less any way that you like. So triangular and square patches are supported, and you can also create a patch that has five points or more.

Because patches can be hooked together in any way that you like, there tends to be a problem with seams appearing in the surface, especially if you are using less regular construction methods. While patches are relatively easy to work with, in the early stages of model-making they do have a tendency to look angular or lumpy. They also require a lot of manual tweaking of points to get them to run smoothly into one another.

Patches that are placed along continuous stretches of a curve are usually fine, but where two unconnected surfaces are hooked together you invariably get a seam or a crease that can prove difficult to remove.

53

2 | 3
This organic form was created from spline patches. You can see that each point on the surface, as well as having a location, has handles that control the shape of the curve going through it. Depending on the number of curves passing through the point there may be four or more handles to control. Each can be moved independently of the others so it's easy to create creases between neighboring patches. Editing spline patch-based models can be tricky, though it varies from program to program.

3

BÉZIER SPLINES AND SURFACES

Some 3D programs have another type of curve that is known as a Bézier curve. These operate in much the same way as they do in 2D programs such as Photoshop and Illustrator. On each point in a Bézier curve there is a tangent handle that allows you to modify the curvature of the curve at that point.

This type of curve offers much more flexibility since you can create smooth, broad curves or sharp curves using a single point. By breaking the tangents you can also create discontinuities in curves, and to do this you need close or overlapping points with traditional splines.

Bézier surfaces also have points with tangent handles. With a single curve there is one pair of handles per point, but on a surface there are two pairs. Though Béziers are flexible, you can end up with a lot of extra surface points to edit—tangent handles, since you have four of these per point, all over the surface.

2

Perspective

1

Bézier curves have points with tangent handles. The top curve has a broad curvature at the selected point because the tangent handles have been extended outward from the point. The center curve has a very sharp curvature at the selected point because the handles are very near to it. The bottom curve has "broken" handles to create a discontinuity, or cusp, in the curve.

54

2
Bézier surfaces have
points that display
two pairs of tangent
handles (the green
dots in the image),
one pair for each
surface direction
u and v (see page 57).

55

Cancel Expert Mode

NURBS

There is a special type of spline that has found favor in 3D graphics due to it having some particularly useful properties. NURBS (Non-Uniform Rational B-Spline) offer greater functionality than Béziers, though at first it may appear that they have less.

NURBS, like simple splines, use control points to define a curve. There are no tangent handles as there are on Béziers. Instead, they have NURBS points, which from here on in we'll refer to as CVs (short for control vertices). These can be weighted to affect the curve at their particular point to a lesser or greater degree.

Part of a NURBS curve's mathematical description is its Degree. A Degree 1 NURBS curve is linear, which means that it has straight segments between each CV. If you raise the degree of a NURBS curve to 2, 3, etc., then the curve becomes smoother. The most common degrees for NURBS are Degree 2 (quadratic) and Degree 3 (cubic).

Understanding the math is not really essential, but it will help if you understand the options you have when working with NURBS. Another difference between NURBS and Bézier curves is that NURBS never pass through their CVs, except (as usually implemented in 3D software) at their end points. The only exception to this is if the NURBS curve is Degree 1 (linear).

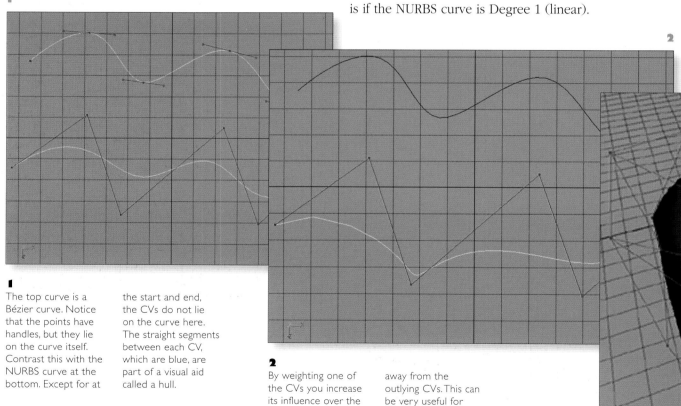

1
The top curve is a Bézier curve. Notice that the points have handles, but they lie on the curve itself. Contrast this with the NURBS curve at the bottom. Except for at the start and end, the CVs do not lie on the curve here. The straight segments between each CV, which are blue, are part of a visual aid called a hull.

2
By weighting one of the CVs you increase its influence over the curve, which pulls closer to it and further away from the outlying CVs. This can be very useful for creating hard edges on NURBS models.

NURBS Primitives can also be created and then sculpted by moving their points. However, unlike polygon objects, whose surface structure can be made up in any way that you like, NURBS surfaces have an extremely rigid topology (surface structure) that is basically like a grid. On a NURBS sphere, each spline curve that defines its surface runs either from pole to pole or parallel to the equator. These two directions of the NURBS surface are called u and v, and are similar to an x, y coordinate system. When editing NURBS surfaces you must move the points because there are no edges or faces as such. That means that you cannot extrude faces or add details to portions of the model in the same way that you can with polygon meshes (or indeed spline patches in some

programs). However, it is possible to add extra detail to the surface by adding a new row or column of CVs in between two others. Of course, the new set of CVs has to go all the way around the model, increasing the point count in places where you may not really need it. This is, fortunately, one of the very few downsides of NURBS surface modeling.

4
You can increase the detail of a NURBS surface by adding an extra row or column of CVs to it. Here an extra row has been added to the object on the right and scaled up to produce a goblet shape.

57

3
With a NURBS object, the CVs lie outside the surface that they control. You can sculpt the surface by moving the CVs, just as with patch surfaces, and you can also weight the CVs.

SUBDIVISION SURFACES 1

There is a geometry type that combines the natural smoothness of NURBS with the ease of use and flexibility of polygons. These are subdivision surfaces, and they offer a simple way to model both organic and mechanical objects with very few compromises.

Subdivision surface modeling works by taking a base model, usually a polygonal model, which is a very rough description of the shape you want to create, and then applying a series of subdivision routines to it that simultaneously smoothes the model and increases its resolution. However, subdivision surface modeling maintains a link between the original, low-resolution polygon mesh and the higher-resolution, smoothed surface. This means that you can continue editing the

2
Once the subdivision is applied, the original low-resolution surface disappears, leaving just a wire-frame cage object with the smoothed surface beneath. Note that the smoothing operation always results in a reduced volume.

2

58

1

1
Here is a low-resolution polygon model (flashlight) before it is converted into a subdivision surface model.

low-resolution polygon surface, using familiar polygon tools, and the smooth surface automatically updates to reflect these changes.

In the same way as for a NURBS model, you can sculpt the smooth surface by moving the points of the polygon control object, but because it is polygonal you can also edit the edges and faces. What is most important is that local refinement of the surface is possible by extending the polygon control cage (for example, extruding a face). The rest of the model is not affected, only the region you extend.

3
You can continue editing the polygon cage object, which in turn modifies the smoothed surface beneath. Here the front of the flashlight is extruded inward.

59

SUBDIVISION SURFACES 2

The other great feature of subdivision surface modeling is that because the cage object is polygonal, you can create models with totally arbitrary topology, unlike the regular u and v patchwork of a NURBS surface. In some of the better subdivision surface implementations you may also use polygon faces that have any number of points. Most current systems limit you by requiring that polygons have only three of four points, but this is a relatively minor restriction considering the other benefits. Some systems let you use n-gons (polygons with an arbitrary "n" number of points) in the polygon control cage. However, many 3D modelers tend to stick with quads because, topologically speaking, it makes modeling easier in the long run.

60

persp

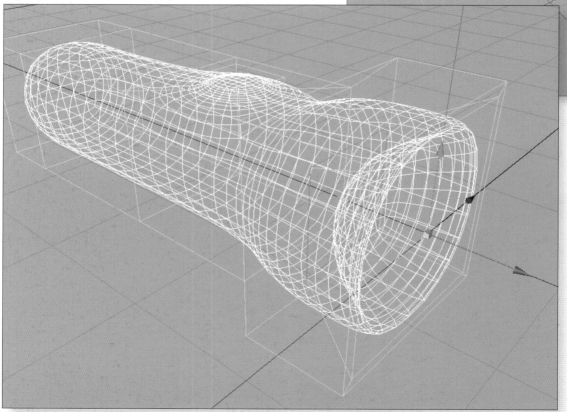

In wire-frame mode you can see the increased resolution of the subdivision process. You can specify the number of iterations that the subdivision process goes through to create an object of the desired resolution. This value can be changed at any time, since the surface is "live."

2 | 3
The end of the flashlight is rounded, a natural result of the smoothing process (*left*). But by selecting the edges at the back of the flashlight you can set them to be a full crease, resulting in a hard edge (*below*).

Like NURBS, subdivision surfaces can be weighted so that sharp creases and edges can be created on otherwise smooth and flowing surfaces. This means that, for example, you don't need to add extra geometry in order to make the edges of a cylinder hard. Both edges and points can be weighted or creased, although not all 3D programs support both options. With those that let you weight points and edges, some let you apply any weighting value while others restrict you to full or partial creasing. Some creasing is better than none, of course.

61

persp

3

GEOMETRY USES

There are no hard-and-fast rules when it comes to choosing which geometry type to use for a particular task, but here are some pointers. For mechanical modeling and illustration or Web design you can use any type of geometry as long as the object looks right.

In CAD/CAM, NURBS and Solid geometry are often used because they can easily and accurately represent the specific shapes and structures that are being created. They can also be analyzed and measured in ways that simple polygon objects can't be, providing the degree of accuracy demanded by the industry.

For character animation, Bézier patches and NURBS are very useful because the surfaces can be deformed without kinking or ripping apart. The low point count also makes them easier to deal with when setting them up for animation. However, creating a detailed bipedal character from a single NURBS surface is almost impossible, so special tools have been designed that enable multiple surfaces to be stitched together. This can cause problems during animation because poor modeling and stitching may result in surfaces literally coming apart at the seams.

In the end, you can use whatever type of geometry you are most comfortable with. Some 3D artists prefer NURBS, while some prefer polygons, but it often depends what industry they work in as well as which toolset they feel most adept at using. Sometimes the extra work involved in getting, for example, a NURBS model to hold together during animation is worth it if the 3D artist feels that he or she is better at modeling using NURBS rather than a simpler geometry type.

62

1
A NURBS object is used to create a model for CAM (Computer Assisted Manufacturing) purposes. One of the properties of NURBS is that the surface curvature can easily be measured.

2

For character animations, subdivision surfaces are ideal. A single skin can be created directly using arbitrary surface topology. The surface is inherently stable—it won't rip or tear, and, in the same way as when using NURBS, a complex character can be built using far fewer points than you would with a polygon mesh. You can also change the resolution of the smoothed surface on the fly (as and when you need it without lots of calculation), speeding the playback of complex scenes.

3

For interactive use, such as in games, polygons are still very much the standard. Polygons are simple, can be rendered directly, and support arbitrary topology.

3

SHADING 1

The end result for the work you do in a 3D program is, most of the time, a 2D image or animation. In order to produce that image, the 3D software has to fill in all the polygons and surfaces you've built to make them appear solid, add in the lighting, calculate any materials and textures you've defined, and process any special effects you might have added. This is a process called rendering and it can take a while to carry out, which is why some understanding of what is going on will pay off if something isn't really looking the way you hoped it would.

Although the mathematics involved are quite complex, some of the concepts are easy to grasp. A cursory understanding of the processes will help you to create better models and images, design better lighting setups, and solve more quickly any problems that you might have.

Shading is the process of filling in the polygons of a 3D mesh object with a color so that objects appear more like they do in the real world, rather than as a mesh of lines and points. There are many different types of shading "models" available in 3D graphics that are suitable for different purposes. The term "model" is used because the shading techniques were designed to model the way light interacts with objects and our eyes to produce an image.

1
Smooth shading shows objects as solids.

2
Textured shading using OpenGL (*see page 66*) is used to show an environmental reflection image on the bottle.

3
Here is the polygon mesh, displayed in all its glory. For a NURBS object this might be the tessellated surface for rendering.

2

3

SHADING 2

Most 3D systems can display fully shaded 3D objects in their viewports, which helps us immensely in visualizing the object. This is thanks to specialized, fast-rendering algorithms that have been developed to be accelerated using hardware. OpenGL, developed by SGI Inc., is the preeminent display rendering technology that is used by today's 3D artists and supported by 3D software. There are other graphics Application Programing Interfaces or APIs, as they are known, such as Heidi, DirectX, and the now little-used QuickDraw 3D. However, it is OpenGL that has become the industry standard for fast 3D displays because of its ability to show smooth shading, textures, and effects in real time on desktop PCs.

Wire-frame views are equally helpful because they allow you to examine the surface structure much more clearly. As you work you will often flip between the two display types, depending on the task at hand. Other display types include Point Cloud, where only the points are displayed; and, for parametric surfaces, there's Isoparms display, which just shows the surface contours (not the tessellated wire-frame surface). Probably the simplest display type, however, is Bounding Box. In this, objects are displayed by a box representing their bounding volume. This is very fast and is good to use on slower systems with more complex scenes, though it's only really useful for testing motion, and maybe composition, if really necessary.

1
Isoparms display used on a NURBS object. Isoparms display is very fast compared to shaded displays, but is only suitable for parametric surfaces and procedural objects.

2
Point Cloud only displays the points. It can be used with all types that have vertices as part of their geometry. It is useful for polygons and parametric surfaces.

3
Bounding Box displays the bounding volume as a simple wire-frame cuboid.

66

2

3

SHADING 3

In order to calculate the color of polygons so that they can be shaded, a virtual light source must initially be defined in the scene. Then the computer is able to calculate what color the polygon will be, based on its angle to the viewpoint and the light source. The most basic type of shading is known as flat shading. Using this technique, each polygon is filled in with a single color, depending on its direction and the location of the light source as well as the light color and intensity. There are other parameters that are taken into account, but that is the basic process, so we'll keep things pared down for now.

The information about the direction of a given polygon is derived from what is known as the Surface Normal—this is the imaginary line that points out from a polygon face and is perpendicular to it. When it comes to flat shading this is all the information that is required, hence the faceted appearance. Another approach, known as Gouraud shading, uses the Normals at the vertex of each polygon in order to gain its information. The color of a facet is then interpolated across the face from the value found at the vertices. This gives a smoothed appearance to the model.

▌ Flat shading fills in each polygon with a single color. This results in a faceted appearance that is fine for previewing but not very convincing for the final output (unless you are creating gemstones or a disco mirror ball).

2

The simplest shading of all is no shading. Objects are filled with a single color with no regard for the directions of the polygon faces.

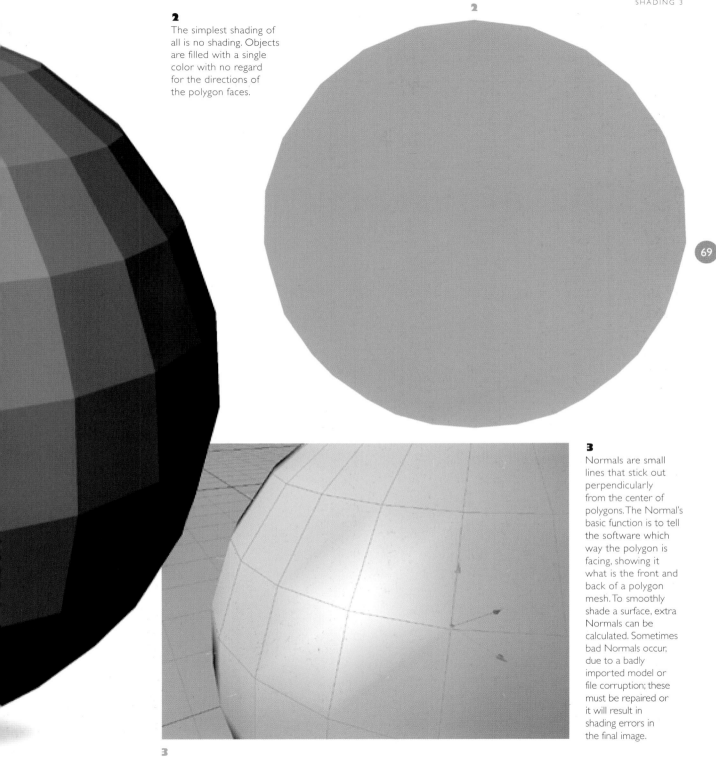

3

Normals are small lines that stick out perpendicularly from the center of polygons. The Normal's basic function is to tell the software which way the polygon is facing, showing it what is the front and back of a polygon mesh. To smoothly shade a surface, extra Normals can be calculated. Sometimes bad Normals occur, due to a badly imported model or file corruption; these must be repaired or it will result in shading errors in the final image.

SHADING 4

These shading algorithms were developed by people who were doing research into computer graphics, and, as a result, they often bear the names of their developers. Some 3D programs offer even more shading types, such as Lambert, which produces smooth shading but without highlights, good for matte surfaces. Other shading algorithms include Blinn shading, which is similar to Phong shading but with more accurate highlights, Oren-Nayer shading, and Cook-Thorrance shading, to name but a few.

1
Gouraud shading averages the colors found at the vertices across the polygon faces, resulting in a smoothing of polygon boundaries. This gets rid of the faceted appearance inherent in flat shading, though there are some problems, such as artifacts, especially on low-resolution models (note the edges of the sphere). Gouraud shading is also not very good at reproducing highlights on objects.

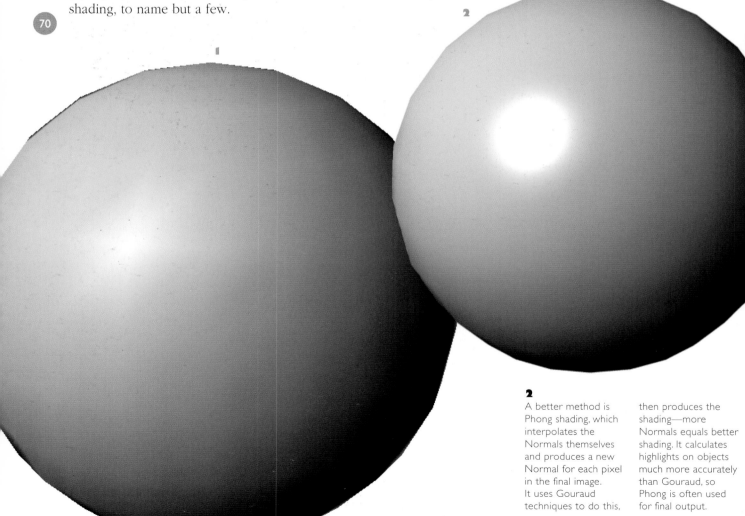

2
A better method is Phong shading, which interpolates the Normals themselves and produces a new Normal for each pixel in the final image. It uses Gouraud techniques to do this, then produces the shading—more Normals equals better shading. It calculates highlights on objects much more accurately than Gouraud, so Phong is often used for final output.

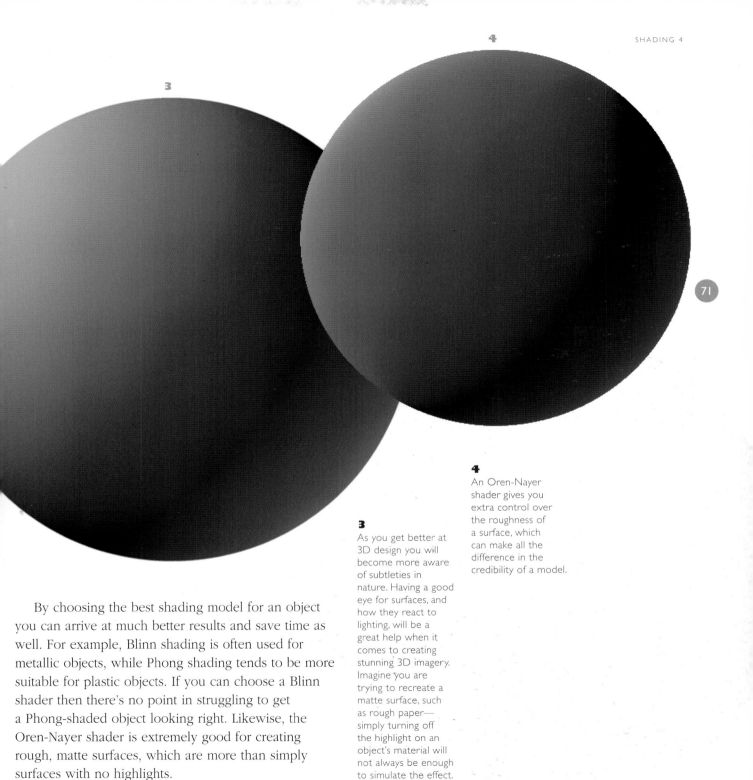

4
An Oren-Nayer
shader gives you
extra control over
the roughness of
a surface, which
can make all the
difference in the
credibility of a model.

3
As you get better at
3D design you will
become more aware
of subtleties in
nature. Having a good
eye for surfaces, and
how they react to
lighting, will be a
great help when it
comes to creating
stunning 3D imagery.
Imagine you are
trying to recreate a
matte surface, such
as rough paper—
simply turning off
the highlight on an
object's material will
not always be enough
to simulate the effect.

By choosing the best shading model for an object
you can arrive at much better results and save time as
well. For example, Blinn shading is often used for
metallic objects, while Phong shading tends to be more
suitable for plastic objects. If you can choose a Blinn
shader then there's no point in struggling to get
a Phong-shaded object looking right. Likewise, the
Oren-Nayer shader is extremely good for creating
rough, matte surfaces, which are more than simply
surfaces with no highlights.

ILLUMINATION

When an object is illuminated by a light source there are three distinct areas to its shading. To see this, get a desk lamp and something shiny, such as an apple, and hold the object under the light. You'll notice that there is a very strong point of light, a hot spot on the apple on the side toward the light. The part of the surface facing away from the light is dark (though not totally black), and in between there is a gradual falloff of shading from the bright hot spot to the side in darkness. This is all due to two basic components of an illuminated surface, the Specular and Diffuse shading. I said there were three main areas to the shading, but only named two. That's because the third is slightly difficult to define. But, although the side of your object opposite to the light is dark, it's not totally black either. This is due to Ambience, or Ambient shading.

Ambient shading is a bit difficult to define. It's the illumination that is produced in an environment by other objects redistributing the light from the main light source. In a room with a window open to the sunshine, even in corners not directly illuminated by the sun you'll notice that it is not totally dark. This ambient light bounces around, illuminating everything, so that nowhere that light can reach is totally black.

To mimic bounced lighting in a computer is very expensive, computationally speaking, so a quick and dirty approximation, called Ambient lighting, is used. It varies from system to system, but most follow a similar method. A global Ambient level is set for the scene, which usually ranges from 0 percent (no illumination) to 100 percent (full illumination). The Ambient shading property of an object can be altered so that it is affected to a greater or lesser degree, just as you can alter the Specular intensity. A higher Ambient shading level on an object makes the unilluminated portions lighter.

By having two controls for Ambient illumination, you can change this portion of the scene lighting globally or for each object. However, Ambient light is just a fudge, and it can make your images look awful. It is usually much better to use low-intensity scene lights to brighten dark areas and simulate ambient lighting than to resort to Ambient light.

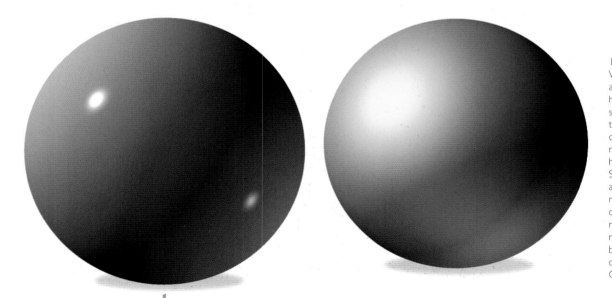

1

When an object is shiny and polished, the Specular highlight is bright and small, but as you roughen the surface it becomes dimmer, broader, and more diffused. As we have seen, turning off the Specular component for a surface makes it appear matte, although you can create even stronger matte surfaces by altering not just the Specular but the Diffuse component, too, as in Oren-Nayer shading.

2

The image above shows a simple scene without any global ambient light.

The areas that are not directly illuminated are totally black.

3

A small amount of Ambient shading lightens the darker area, but also seems to be impacting the quality of the image. There is a lack of contrast to the image that looks quite unlike the effect of real ambient light.

73

4

A high Ambient level has totally destroyed the shading in the image, rendering it flat and lifeless. Notice that in the top left corner of the room you can't make out any difference in the illumination between the two walls.

4

SPECULARITY

Strictly speaking, all objects are reflective. This means that they return to the environment some of the light that they receive. Much of the light is diffused—the light penetrates the surface and bounces around before emerging at some odd angle. This is why the term Diffuse reflections is used when describing this property. Specular reflections are produced when the angle of reflection equals the angle of incidence. This is shown in the diagram below.

The reflection effect we are used to in a 3D application is simply referring to returned light from a surface that has not been sufficiently diffused so that a recognizable image can be discerned. Specular reflections are reflected images just the same—images of the bright light source.

Because lights don't really "glow" in a 3D program you really need to have a Specularity control in order to fake the effect—unless you set up a visible luminous object where your light is and render it with raytraced reflections, but this is overkill. However, having said that, there are techniques that involve creating specular highlights with reflected geometry, and these are especially useful when a light source is spread over a wide area, such as a window.

The two gray lines represent light rays that have been diffused by the surface so that its incoming and outgoing angles, relative to the surface, are not the same (producing Diffuse illumination). The red line represents a ray producing a Specular highlight from the camera's point of view. This ray's incoming and outgoing angles are equal, relative to the surface. As you can see, a Specular highlight appearing on an object's surface is dependent on the relative positions of the light and the camera. That is why the Specular highlight on an object appears to move when you move your viewpoint (or the light, for that matter).

Camera

Light

Object

Sometimes shading models are built into an application's rendering engine (the part of the program that generates the image), and in other systems it is possible to apply different shading models on an object-by-object basis. These add-ons to the rendering engine are known as Shaders because they effect the shading process. However, many rendering systems let you plug into all parts of the rendering pipeline in order to create many different effects, and the term "Shader" can be applied to any piece of code that modifies the rendering process. Shaders can be illumination models, as we've seen on the previous pages (*see pages 72–73*), texture generators, light effects, or camera lenses. It is also possible to have Utility Shaders that measure a certain property of a surface and pass it onto another Shader for some other operation, like controlling the amount of transparency.

2
This image of a reflective sphere was created using a 100 percent luminous window model to provide the Specular highlight. The model is made from just four polygons, and raytracing (*see page 88*) was used to make it reflect in the sphere's surface. A light was positioned in front of the window model to provide illumination for the scene.

75

USING IMAGE MAPS

The great trick with 3D graphics is that it is possible to take an image, painted by hand or photographed, and then wrap it around an object. If the image is of a plank of wood, then the finished object will appear to have a wooden surface. Use a photo of a rusty metal plate and your object will look like a rusted metal plate. A combination of clever modeling and texture maps can be used to imply a great deal of detail without actually having to build it.

Image maps are very useful, though getting a certain look is not always quite that simple. All objects have a number of different properties that make them look like what they are. Wood has a color pattern (the grain), which can be captured in a photo, but it also has certain shading properties that cannot be captured and fed into the computer using a photograph.

If the wood is from a palette or crate, for example, it is likely to be very rough and have few or no specular highlights. It may also have a textured or bumpy surface that can't be directly photographed. These parameters must be set up in a material definition by the artist, but the key to getting the look right is being able to identify these properties or qualities in the first place.

The wood image is an ordinary RGB (the red, green, and blue components that make up a full-color image on a computer) file that is used to determine the color of the object at each pixel. However, other factors, such as the color of the light source and the shading model, contribute too. What the RGB image really does is define a raw base color for the object. Of course, if you put this object in a different scene with different settings, the object will look slightly different, but it will still have the basic wood pattern.

76

1

2

1|2
An image of a piece of wood has been wrapped around this sphere and used as the color portion of the object's material definition. It looks as if it is made of wood, but it is not entirely convincing.

We can use image maps to drive other material parameters, too. Bump mapping is one of the most important uses for image maps and, along with the color map, goes a long way toward fooling the eye into believing that it is seeing a real object. A bump map needs to be a grayscale image of the texture that you want to simulate. Although the wood image is in color, you can take it to a 2D paint program, such as Photoshop, and then turn it into a grayscale image for use as a bump map. Because the bump map is derived from the color map, the features in both will line up, which further adds to the effect. Using the color map for the bumps does not provide an accurate description of the surface texture of the wood, but is often used, especially if time is of the essence.

3
The RGB wood image is duplicated and converted to a grayscale image and is then saved.

3

When it is rendered with a bump map, the surface of the sphere displays a grain texture just as if it were the real grain. The relief is an effect that is produced by carefully manipulating the interpolated Surface Normals pixel by pixel. Precisely how this technique works is not really important, but what is important is the relationship between the shades of gray in the bump-map image and the effect that you see rendered. Basically, white areas in the grayscale wood image produce highs or ridges on a surface, while the black areas produce lows or grooves. In between there is a smooth graduation in height. This effect is caused by playing with the Normals so that they aren't really bumps, geometrically speaking. Extracting the grayscale information from an RGB

78

5
To make the bumps more prominent you can increase the specularity of the surface. Now it looks as if it has received a coat of varnish, but you can see the effect of the bump map more clearly. Notice how the black lines in the image appear as deep grooves.

4
When applied to the bump channel of the material, the grayscale image produces a texture or relief on the surface. Areas that are black in the image represent low points and areas that are white are high points.

4

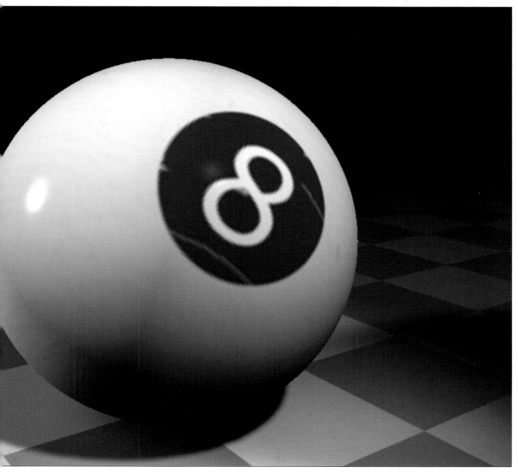

image is the simplest way to get a bump map, since you can't photograph such things in reality. However, you can also use the RGB image directly in many 3D programs as a bump map without first having to convert it to grayscale. The program will do the conversion internally at render time, though, for better control over the end result, you will probably want to do it yourself.

A better way to capture a surface's texture is to take a rubbing or an imprint of it. 3D artists have been known to cover their own faces with a light coating of ink or paint and then press it onto a piece of paper in order to extract their own skin bump textures!

By changing the color and bump maps applied to the sphere pictured, you can turn it into a different object entirely. As mentioned, you can use photographs for image maps, but you can also create them from scratch. By painting image maps you can create any kind of object look you want, be it realistic or totally stylized.

6 | 7
By replacing the color and bump maps for the sphere with the eight-ball color and bump maps, a pool ball was created instead.

79

CONTROLLING MATERIAL CHANNEL INTENSITY

Color and bump mapping are special cases as far as image maps go, but all the other properties that a material possesses can also be controlled with a map. Transparency, reflection, specular intensity, luminosity, and Diffuse channels can all be controlled using an image map, for example. In all these cases, though, the image map serves to vary the intensity of the channel across the object's surface, and, in the same way as for bump maps, black equals a low effect, white equals a high effect, and shades of gray produce a variation in between.

The following five examples show the effect of a single-texture black-and-white map as it is applied to each of an object's material channels in turn.

1
This is the texture that was used, a mottled black-and-white image. The strong contrast should show off the effect well. Remember that it is the image that controls the effect. Wherever the image is white, the channel is at 100 percent intensity; where it is black, it is at 0 percent intensity. Note that in each of the subsequent pictures the image is wrapped around the sphere in the same way each time.

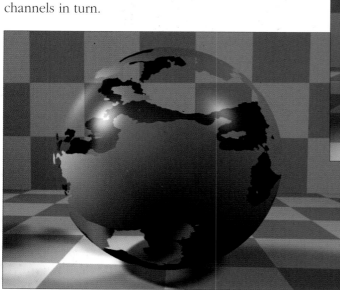

3
Image applied to the Reflectivity channel.

2
Image applied to the Transparency channel.

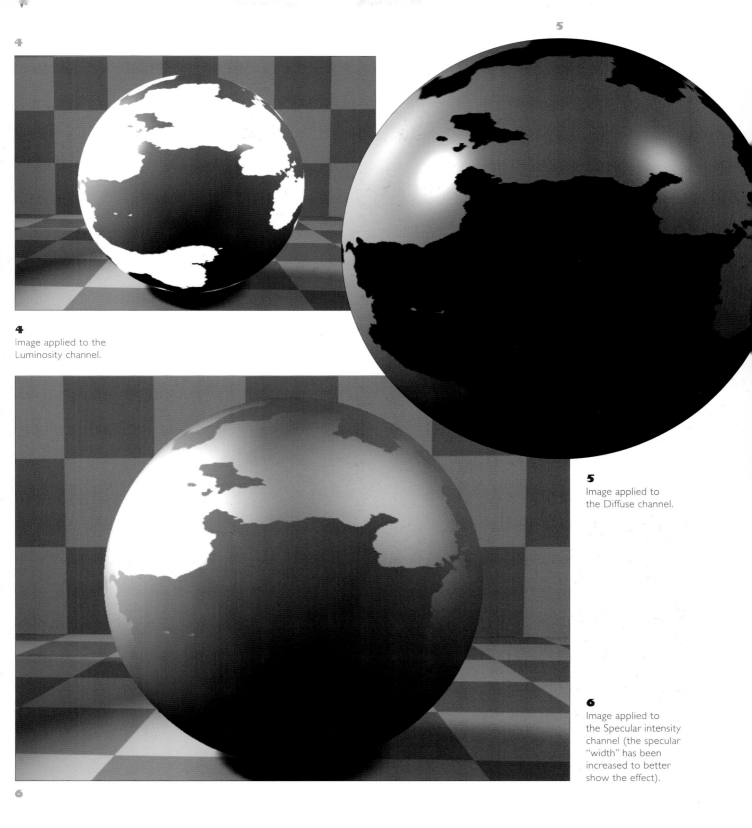

4

4
Image applied to the
Luminosity channel.

5

5
Image applied to
the Diffuse channel.

6
Image applied to
the Specular intensity
channel (the specular
"width" has been
increased to better
show the effect).

6

BUMPS VERSUS DISPLACEMENT

2

Bump mapping is an effect, a virtual trick of the light. The surface of the object does not change at all—it is only the shading of the object that is modified in order to give the impression of texture or relief.

Bump mapping is good for small details, such as the pits in a golf ball, the grooves in wooden floorboards, skin and scales, brickwork, and so on. However, larger surface details are better modeled rather than bump-mapped because the trick will become obvious at some angles.

82

1

1 | 2

Here is a bump map that has been applied to a sphere. When you are not too close, the bumps look convincing enough, but if you zoom up to the edge you'll notice that it is perfectly flat. If these were truly bumps the silhouette would also be bumpy. You'll also notice that the bumps tend to look distorted, too.

3
A displacement map
was used instead of
a bump map here.
Notice that the edge
of the sphere is
bumpy because these
are real bumps.

There is a way to create real
bumps on surfaces—by using
displacement mapping. In the same
way as in bump mapping, a
grayscale image is used to define
high and low areas. However, this
time the information is used to
move the points on a polygon mesh
surface in the direction of the
polygon Surface Normals so that the
surface becomes bumpy. In order
for displacement mapping to work
well you must have a lot of
polygons, because the detail is
limited by how finely subdivided the
surface is. However, by combining
bump mapping and displacement
mapping you can arrive at a very
realistic, detailed look.

ENVIRONMENT MAPPING

Raytraced reflections are accurate but they can take a long time to render (*see page 88*). You can fake reflectivity by using image maps, just as you can use them to fake bumps, color, or any other property.

By applying an image of an environment, such as a landscape or a room, and projecting it onto an object from an imaginary sphere that surrounds it, it appears as though the object is reflecting its environment. No rays need to be cast since it's just a shading technique, so it is very fast to calculate. Because the projection sphere is

infinitely large and not actually connected to an object, as the reflective object moves and rotates in the scene the environment image moves over its surface, distorting as it does so, just like a real reflection would.

Environment reflection maps can be used to great effect on all objects that require reflections. They work especially well for objects that are not highly reflective since the minor limitations are not visible. For very reflective objects, where accuracy is important, raytracing is the better option.

84

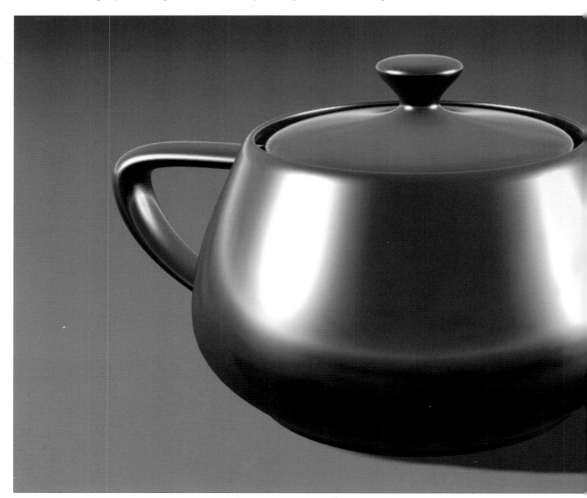

∎
Here an environment image map has been used to simulate reflections on this teapot. Despite there being nothing else in this scene, the object appears quite convincingly reflective, and it did not take long to render.

Light&Blue 360.img (RGB 1:1)

(819, 228):(157, 137, 138)

85

There are numerous ways in which to create environment maps. You can paint them yourself in Photoshop or, to render a scene built specifically for this purpose, in a 3D program using a QuickTime Panoramic render. By far the easiest way is to use photographs scanned into your computer (from an image CD or from the Web) that can be edited in Photoshop so that they work better as environment maps. The main reason for this is to remove the seams that occur as the image is wrapped around the projecting sphere.

Some programs, such as ElectricImage (*see page 19 and page 26*), generate environment maps from the 3D scene itself. It does this by rendering six images from the center of the reflective object in six directions (top, bottom, front, back, left, and right). These images are then reapplied as an environment map using a cubic projection. With a little bit of effort a similar effect can be achieved in most 3D programs, although the process is manually intensive.

2
This is the environment image map used to create the reflection. It is a landscape generated in a 360° panoramic image from another 3D program.

RENDERING

Rendering is one of the most confusing and misunderstood aspects of 3D computer graphics. There is so much misinformation and generalization, and so many plain old untruths told by both users and companies, that some effort should be made in this book to clarify the chaos.

The word rendering itself covers a wide gamut of uses, but for our purposes two broad categories can be defined. The first is interactive rendering— this encompasses all the rendering methods and technologies that display 3D imagery as quickly as possible to provide the viewer with feedback of the 3D information as instantly as possible. The shaded view in your 3D application or games console provides such "display" rendering, which is (more often than not) hardware-accelerated. The other criterion for this heading is that the rendering is not, and often can't be, saved to a file but is jettisoned every time the image is redrawn.

2
Final-quality rendering is produced by software. These images are saved to disk after completion and can take a while to produce. (Pixar, the company that produced *Toy Story*, calculated that if a film was to be completed in a year, each frame should take, on average, two minutes to produce.) Some final-quality hardware rendering systems are available, such as RenderDrive from ART, but they are rare.

1
The shaded view you see in your 3D application is displayed on the fly by your computer's 3D graphics card, together with a rendering technology such as OpenGL.

3
Final-quality rendering is used to create the images and effects in movies, video, and feature segments (FMVs or full motion video) in computer games. *The Matrix* is a good example of photo-realistic software rendering.

4
The 3D imagery you see when you play a computer game is drawn to the screen in real time by sophisticated hardware. This is either a dedicated 3D graphics card in your computer or a games console.

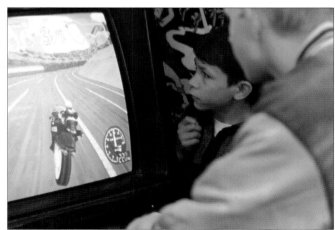

The other category can be called final-quality rendering or (the often misused) photo-real rendering. This is usually done by software alone for video, film, or print. The goal here is quality (i.e. free from artifacts, such as shading errors, aliasing, etc.), not interactivity, and the images are usually saved to disk as image files.

From these descriptions, one of the first misunderstandings can be dispelled: that 3D graphics cards are anything to do with final rendering. They aren't. All that a top-of-the-line 3D workstation gets you is faster display rendering. It's up to the CPU (and memory and other subsystems) to provide the horsepower that propels a final render. That said, there are exceptions. Alias|Wavefront's Maya, for example, requires many of its particle effects to be saved using hardware rendering. In fact, there's nothing inherent in OpenGL (or Direct3D, etc.) that says it can only be used for interactive display applications; it's simply that these technologies have been developed for such uses and are therefore optimized to do them. If you want the quickest 3D display you'll probably use hardware-accelerated OpenGL or Direct3D. If you want the highest-quality image from your 3D application with the least fuss, then it is best to use the software render engine that was specifically developed for that purpose.

RAYTRACING

Over the years, many methods have been devised that simulate the properties of light and materials in the quest to produce realistic imagery on the computer. Computers use these rendering algorithms to draw 3D objects that look convincingly real. The most intuitive approach is to have the computer simulate what happens to light in the real world using the physics of optics. This is the principle of raytracing, whereby individual rays of light are traced as they traverse the scene from the light source to the viewpoint. The initial problem with this "forward raytracing," as it is known, is that many of the rays that leave a light source never actually end up at the viewpoint at all, but are scattered into the void. Having the computer calculate the paths of millions of never-to-be-seen light rays is computationally wasteful, but there is a useful alternative. Rather than starting the rays off at the light, it is better to start them

off at the point of view and follow them backward (through each pixel of the image-to-be) to the light.

In raytracing, all of the hard-to-fake optical properties we expect to see in a photo-real image, such as shadows, reflection and refraction, naturally fall out of the technique. To calculate reflectivity, therefore, the initial primary ray generates a secondary ray when it hits a surface tagged as reflective. This second ray then bounces off in another direction, until it either vanishes out of the scene (in which case the ray returns the scene background color, assuming the object is 100 percent reflective) or hits another object in the scene. If it hits an object it will obviously return that object's color instead. Many programs have safety measures in place to stop highly recursive (or even infinite) ray generation occurring, usually in the form of a "maximum ray-depth setting." The problem with raytracing is that it is computationally intensive and, for very complex scenes, is not really practical. This is because of the large number of primary rays that are needed to determine which faces in the scene are visible. Because raytracing is slow it is never used for interactive display rendering—that may change when CPUs get fast enough, though.

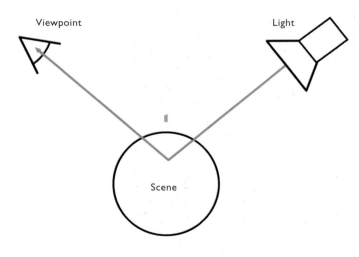

1

In raytracing, an imaginary ray of light is traced from the light source through the scene and back to the viewpoint. For a basic calculation one ray of light is traced for each pixel in the final image. This doesn't produce a very good image, however, and in order to get satisfactory quality many more light rays are traced.

2

This image of a glass has been rendered with no transparency or reflection. It's not at all glasslike, mostly because we expect to see a drinking glass that is transparent.

3

In this image transparency and reflection have been added. The glass has become more like what we expect to see in the real world, but it doesn't look entirely convincing.

89

4

With refraction turned on, as well as transparency and reflection, the glass instantly looks much more credible. With refraction, the thin walls of the glass bend the light slightly so that what you see through the glass is not what lies exactly behind it from the viewing direction.

4

SCANLINE RENDERING

The scanline renderer progresses one line of pixels at a time, displayed here with a white line.

The scanline approach to rendering applies a different method to those previously described. Rather than getting bogged down with total physical accuracy, it paints in the polygons using optimized shading algorithms (Lambert, Gouraud, Phong, Blinn, etc.). This type of rendering usually progresses one line of pixels at a time, hence the name scanline rendering.

After the renderer has depth-sorted the scene to find out which faces are visible and need to be shaded, these algorithms are used to literally fill in the polygons, taking into account the lighting and material definitions. Depth-sorting may actually still be done using simplified raytracing, which is sometimes called ray casting because only the primary rays are used—one for each pixel. Alternatively, a Z-Buffer sorting algorithm can be employed. This furnishes each polygon in the scene with a value, depending on its distance from the camera. If a given pixel contains overlapping polygons in its line of sight, then their values are read, and only the polygon with the highest Z-Buffer value (the closest to the camera) is shaded. The result of all these technical shenanigans is that rendering times are vastly reduced, especially when compared to raytracing.

The problem with the scanline rendering method is that effects such as reflection, refraction, and shadows are not calculated automatically. It is possible to simulate reflection and shadow casting using special tricks, but a refraction effect can be much more difficult to achieve with a fake.

Therefore, many renderers employ a hybrid of scanline rendering and raytracing. In this case, raytracing is evoked only for pixels that contain reflective or refractive polygons. In this way you seem to be able to get the best of both worlds.

Reflectivity is easily faked by using environmental image maps, and shadows can also be easily and quickly produced by rendering a special grayscale image from the point of view of the light to determine occlusion (and therefore determine where the shadows are). Many experienced 3D artists as well as novices make the mistake of assuming that a raytracer is inherently better than a scanline-based renderer. This is a huge mistake to make.

It usually requires only a small amount of extra setup and effort by an artist to get a scanline renderer to produce photo-real shadows and reflections, and the time-saving when raytracing means it is almost always worthwhile. In fact, the most prolific, and arguably the best, commercial rendering engine in use today does not raytrace. Pixar's Photorealistic RenderMan, used to produce the majority of 3D-rendered imagery you see in motion pictures, is very, very quick and produces stunning images, but it does not raytrace.

90

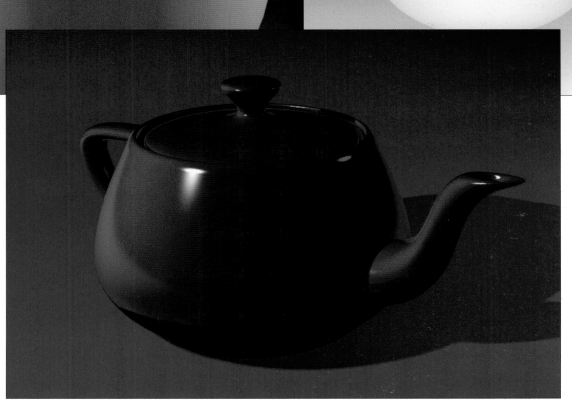

2
This is what a
depth map looks
like. It was rendered
automatically by the
software from the
light casting the
shadow.

3
This is the image
using the depth-
map shadow.

3

RADIOSITY

Radiosity is a technique that attempts physical accuracy with regard to lighting. Its purpose is to describe the energy distribution in a scene by effectively making every object a potential light source. In the real world, when light strikes an object, part of the light is absorbed and the rest is reflected back into the environment. This reflected light carries on through the scene, striking other objects until its energy has been completely absorbed (possibly ending its passage at your retina, which results in you seeing the object). This is why light streaming into a window illuminates not only the opposite wall, but under and between objects and into corners. It's not the direct light that is doing this, but rather the reflected light from walls and objects in the room.

It is reflected light that radiosity simulates. Radiosity describes the reflected light distribution in a scene, and then, usually another rendering method, often raytracing, is used to actually render the image, taking into account the radiosity information. There are a few methods for achieving this, but generally they all require a great deal of computation time, much more so than standard raytracing. The technological details of the different radiosity methods are beyond the scope of this book, but the examples shown here will help to demonstrate the effect that a radiosity calculation will have on a 3D scene.

1
The raytraced image is provided for reference. Notice that it lacks the lighting detail and naturalness of the radiosity render. An area outside the cone of the spotlight 's direct illumination remains black.

1

2
Adaptive radiosity calculates the effect of bounced light radiation in a scene between objects, but is much quicker than the full radiosity method. Notice the color of the red sphere bleeding onto the floor and the way that the shadow is not totally black in some areas but is illuminated by reflected light from nearby surfaces. A single spotlight is all that is used to light the scene.

3

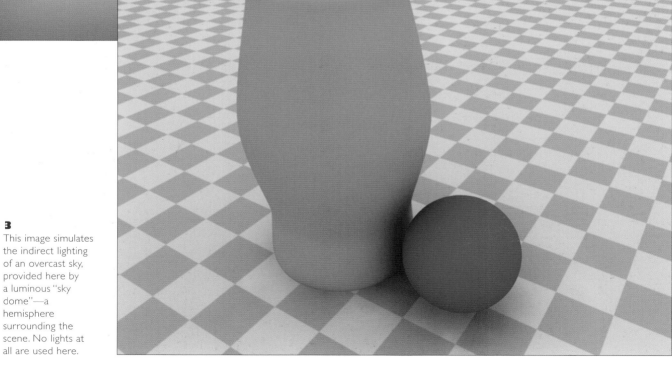

3
This image simulates the indirect lighting of an overcast sky, provided here by a luminous "sky dome"—a hemisphere surrounding the scene. No lights at all are used here.

94

MODELING

Learning 3D digital design is fun. It's difficult at times, but incredibly rewarding in the end. So what better way to learn about the tips and tricks of applied 3D computer graphics than with some hands-on examples? In this section, we'll look at the basics first, explore the more advanced possibilities, and then examine the difficulties that you might encounter day-to-day when producing 3D work.

There are many different technologies for creating 3D objects, the most simple and straightforward of these being the polygon. This is the simplest type of geometry in 3D graphics. It is flexible, robust, and easy to render, but not without its limitations. NURBS are special, mathematically defined surfaces that are constructed from a net of curves. Unlike polygons, they can represent smooth surfaces without requiring hundreds of points, but are quite inflexible in their surface structure and therefore require a specialized toolset.

1
A mesh of connected points forms the polygon object's surface. On the left is a polygon object constructed from myriad polygons that only approximates the curved surface. Polygons are flat, so using them to define any curved surface is like trying to draw a circle using straight lines. On the right is a NURBS object that uses mathematical equations to define the surface, which results in a smooth, accurate model. The purple lines are called hulls and link the NURBS control points to provide a visual clue to the way the points are linked up.

1

persp

2

Close inspection of the two surfaces reveals their differences. The polygon surface on the left looks choppy in profile because of the flat nature of polygons. The NURBS object, however, appears smooth, no matter how close you get to it.

TESSELLATION

To display NURBS surfaces as lit and shaded objects, 3D programs would have to tessellate them first. Tessellation means "to tile," so it's the approximation of a surface using polygon "tiles," usually triangles. Unlike a simple polygon object, a NURBS surface can have its tessellated resolution changed on the fly. So, as you work, you may have a lower tessellation, giving you a good but rough feedback of the curvature of the surface—enough for constructing the scene or animating—but the tessellation can be made much finer when the surfaces are rendered.

A benefit of tessellating NURBS surfaces in order to render them is that it can be done dynamically, depending on the surfaces' distance from the camera. If the object is far away it doesn't require so many polygons to look okay, but as you approach it the tessellation can increase, so that even if you zoom right into the surface you'll never see a facet. The corollary to this is that dynamically tessellated objects minimize system resources during rendering, particularly memory requirements, because the further away they are, the less data is required in their construction.

Imagine a fleet of spacecraft, perhaps a hundred or more, flying through space. The camera follows the group, skirting its outer edge, until it finally flies off into the distance. If NURBS are used to construct the ship model, dynamic tessellation means that the ships close to the camera will be highly tessellated, ships in the mid-distance will have a medium tessellation, while the most distant (the majority) will have a low tessellation. You will save time making this imagery using tessellations because you won't have to build three separate models of different resolutions, or have the hassle of making sure the right models are in the right places at the right times.

1

NURBS surfaces are tessellated into polygons for display and rendering. The polygons are only an approximation of the true NURBS surface, but the resolution of the tessellation can be as fine as you like, down to the subpixel level if you wish, but for any given image it produces the appearance of a perfect surface. Most of the time, subpixel tessellation is not necessary since the polygons here are quite large, but the object is well described by them. Note that triangles are used for the tessellation. This is because triangles can never be bent or ill-formed like quadrangles or other polygons, so they will render perfectly.

PARAMETRIC OBJECTS

Parametric objects are another geometry type. Well, they are not strictly a type of geometry in the same way that polygons or NURBS are; instead, they are a way of creating geometry and maintaining control over the parameters. Parametric models are like mini programs or mathematical formulas that create 2D and 3D objects within the host 3D program. The objects that they create could be made of polygons, NURBS, or any other sort of geometry, but what is unique about parametric models is that the parameters can be edited to change the resulting object's shape. This is similar in a way to construction history, except that with a

1
The parametric cube object above has not had any changes made to its basic shape.

2
By accessing the cube's parameters you can modify them to, for example, increase the number of polygons used to make it up. This is useful because you may want to deform the object and so will need a higher resolution to keep the deformation smooth.

parametric object all the input parameters are already supplied and cannot be changed. For example, a parametric sphere may have controls for radius but also for sweep, allowing you to create a hemisphere or segment. A parametric cube may have controls for the number of subdivisions each face has, or whether or not the edges are to be rounded.

Parametric objects vary from program to program since the number of parameters given to a parametric object and the output geometry type is up to the programmers. They may even provide you with a choice of geometry.

It is usually possible to convert a parametric object into standard geometry, say, a polygonal cube or sphere, thereby losing all the input parameters that can change its shape. This may be necessary in order to edit the object on a component level—for example, to edit the surface CVs (control vertices, *see pages 56–57*) if it is a NURBS object, trim it, or add or subtract surface isoparms and project curves onto it.

3
These four shapes have been created from the same parametric Primitive. By simply changing the settings you can arrive at totally different shapes, though the amount of variability depends on the parameters that are offered by the Primitive.

4
Another way to generate 3D surfaces is by using formulas. An option offered in some 3D programs is almost like creating your own parametric Primitives using mathematical functions. Here a sinusoidal curve has been created using a formula entered into the object's parameter control panel.

SURFACES VERSUS SOLIDS

So far, we've looked at 3D objects that can be constructed from surfaces, such as nets of either polygons or NURBS curves. A flat NURBS plane has two sides, like a piece of paper; if you curl the surface in both axes to form a sphere you still have two sides—it's just that one is inside and the other outside. A sphere created in this way from NURBS or polygons is hollow because it's simply a surface surrounding a region of 3D space.

Another way to represent closed volumes is by using parametric objects called Solids. Solid objects do not have two sides and they can never be open. In other words, they always enclose a volume, no matter what their actual shape is. While there's no way to unwrap a Solid, there are special cases, such as infinite planes, which are open but still one-sided.

The other aspect of Solids is that they have no control points—their surface is entirely analytically defined. That means that you can't sculpt them in the same way as you can a surface with points, but it also means that the object's resolution is infinitely fine. You can slice and dice a Solid as much as you like, with no degradation or risk of the object falling to pieces.

Solids are particularly well suited to industrial modeling tasks such as CAD/CAM and product visualization. This is why many of the packages geared toward these fields feature Solid geometry engines at their core. NURBS

technology is also used in these programs since you'll need to be able to create open surfaces, such as car body panels. Programs that combine surfaces and solids have a problem, though: because of the inherent differences in the geometry types there needs to be tools for each. This can make it confusing, since it's not always obvious if a given object is a Solid or Surface. There are exceptions—ElectricImage Universe features a hybrid surface/solid modeling environment, but also a common toolset.

2
Here is a Solid before it is cut with the Knife tool. A Knife is exactly like its real world counterpart, though maybe cheese wire is a more appropriate comparison. There are Knife tools available that are circular or square, and ones that even use a curve.

1
If you take a Solid sphere and a Surface sphere and then cut them down the middle, you get two different kinds of objects. It's the same as cutting a basketball and a ball of cheese in half: one is hollow and the other is not. The basketball has two sides, but the cheese has only one side, its outside. You can replicate most solid objects using Surfaces, but you cannot represent an open surface using Solids.

3
After a number of cuts the object has become very complex, yet it is still well formed and ready for more.

4

4
This time some of the edges that have been cut into the block are rounded off. If this were a polygon object it would be nearly impossible to round off such complex edges, but the Solid has little difficulty.

CREATING A PISTON USING SOLID MODELING

The best way to show Solid modeling is by demonstration. In this example we will create a mechanical part, a piston, using the Solid modeling in ElectricImage Modeler, a robust application that uses the renowned ACIS geometry kernel from Spatial Corporation.

1

Begin with a Solid Cylinder Primitive, which is duplicated and scaled down slightly. This is positioned so that it protrudes from the base of the larger cylinder, ready for a Boolean Subtraction *(see pages 110–13 for an explanation of this).*

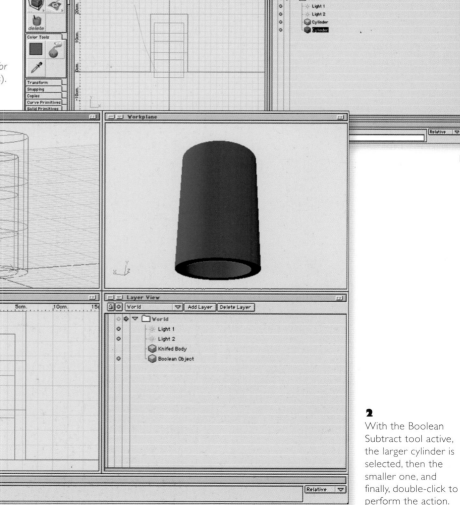

1

2

With the Boolean Subtract tool active, the larger cylinder is selected, then the smaller one, and finally, double-click to perform the action.

2

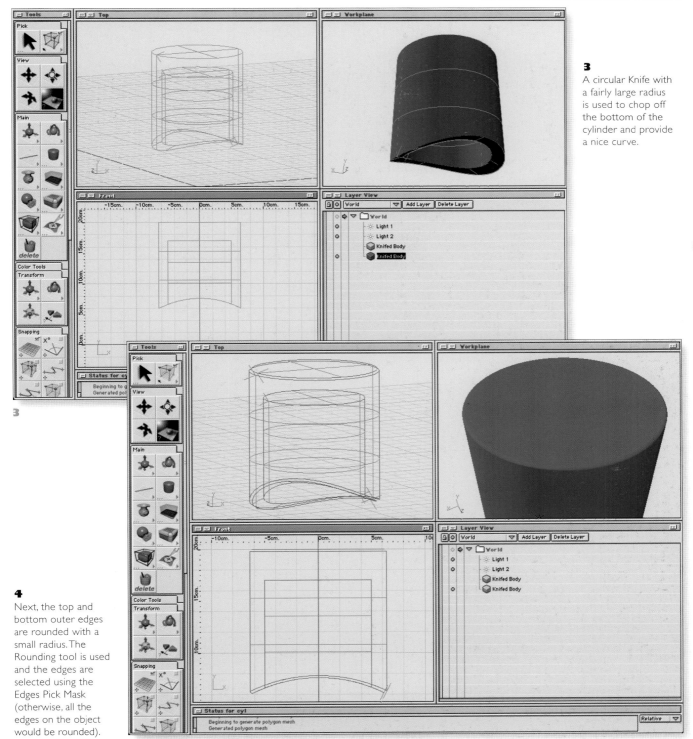

3
A circular Knife with a fairly large radius is used to chop off the bottom of the cylinder and provide a nice curve.

4
Next, the top and bottom outer edges are rounded with a small radius. The Rounding tool is used and the edges are selected using the Edges Pick Mask (otherwise, all the edges on the object would be rounded).

5

Next, three more objects were created—another cylinder and two toruses. The new cylinder was positioned to intersect the old one at its center, and the toruses were created with a primary radius (ring) just slightly smaller than the main cylinder and with a very small secondary radius (the pipe radius). (The second torus is just a duplicate of the first one.)

6

The three new objects are duplicated, grouped into a new layer, and hidden. Then another Boolean Subtract is used. The main cylinder is picked first, then each subsequent object is picked (one each of the ungrouped toruses and cylinder) and designated as the subtraction objects. Here's the result of the subtraction.

7

The duplicated subtraction objects are unhidden (the cylinder is cut down by knifing each end) and scaled down slightly, as if they fitted in the subtracted areas perfectly. The cylinder could have been scaled along its length, but the version of ElectricImage Modeler used here did not support non-uniform scaling at that time.

8

The rest of the piston was modeled in a similar fashion using Boolean Union and knifing to form the shaft. It was then all rounded to blend the parts together.

PRIMITIVE MODELING

Because 3D programs provide you with a bunch of Primitive objects, simply assembling them in the right combinations is the easiest way to model. Of course, primitive modeling does have its limitations, so it is only really suited for simple objects that do not require a lot of realism.

1

2

3

To create four legs you can either duplicate the cube or copy and paste it three times. The best option is to create instances of the cube. An instance is a reference to the original object, not a complete copy, using the duplicate modeling function in XL. If you change the original, the instances change too, but you can also move, distort, or change the instances independently.

1 | 2

The simplest modeling procedure uses Primitives to build an object, which, in this case, is a table. Begin with a cube using Cinema 4D XL from Maxon Computer, then scale it in the y axis to form a table leg. To scale an object you can use a Scale tool and drag on one of the on-screen transform gizoms, or you can deactivate the z and x axes and drag anywhere. For precise scaling you can enter a scale value in the objects' numeric coordinates panel.

3

4
Using instances makes the legs look a bit harsh, so you can round off their edges, too. By using instances, all you have to do to add rounding is change the original leg cube.

5 | 6
The tabletop is added, which is another cube. It is scaled in z and x so that it just overlaps the legs and is positioned so that it sits on top of them. Now you can add rounded edges to the tabletop; because the cubes are parametric Primitives instead of just polygons or NURBS, it is possible to access the cubes' parameters to add the rounding, without having to perform a complicated modeling procedure or rebuilding the top from scratch.

BOOLEANS

Boolean modeling is a technique that uses objects as cutting tools. You can use Booleans to subtract one shape from another, to unify two shapes, or to intersect two shapes. It's similar to adding, subtracting, and intersecting selections in Photoshop, except that it obviously occurs in 3D.

1 | 2 | 3
Here is a simple Boolean modeling operation. A sphere and torus are added to the scene and the torus is positioned so that it intersects the sphere at its equator (1). With the Boolean tool set to Subtract, the torus removes a part of the sphere, leaving the part that was intersecting it behind (2). If you change the order of the operation, you get the opposite: the sphere is subtracted from the torus (3).

110

1

2

3

4

An option in some programs is to cut the surfaces rather than subtract them. In this case, the torus cuts away part of the sphere, as before, but does not leave its imprint in the surface.

5

Intersecting the two objects produces an object that is made of only the parts of the two objects that overlapped—i.e. where they intersect each other in 3D.

1

1
A Boolean intersection creates an object that is equal to the portions of the two objects that overlapped. The order of the objects is not important in this case. Intersections can be used to create interesting compound objects like the one shown here, which is formed by a cone and a capsule.

2
Booleans are usually created between polygon objects, though NURBS can be Booleaned too. The problem with Booleans is that where the two objects intersect, the edges produced are liable to artifacting (such as shading errors, aliasing, etc.), especially if the objects aren't made up of enough polygons in the first place.

2

3
By increasing the resolutions of the Boolean objects, the edges are much cleaner and artifact-free. The disadvantage is that you end up with much denser objects, but in many circumstances this is a small price to pay, because Boolean objects can be fiendishly difficult to recreate any other way.

4
Another problem with polygonal Booleans is that they result in edges that are, frankly, a mess. Though they look fine rendered, the sheer number of points along Boolean edges means that it is difficult to do anything with them afterward.

ECONOMICAL MODELING 1

114

1
When planning an animation it can be a good idea to make a few sketches that lay out the action and camera angles. These drawings are called storyboards.

2
A storyboard doesn't have to be well drawn; like this one, it just needs to provide you with a plan of attack. Usually, the mere act of producing a storyboard forces you to plan each shot.

When modeling objects that will eventually be used in an animation, it is always best to make a plan so that you know what will be seen in the final animation, and, therefore, what you need to model to get the desired result. It is a very good idea to create a storyboard. A storyboard is a series of sketches that depict key moments in an animation. What a storyboard will also contain is a rough guide to the camera positions and directions so that at each important moment you get a good idea of what will be in a shot and what will not. The golden rule of modeling should be adhered to at all times: model only what will actually be visible in the animation.

3

3
When you draw a storyboard you may find that a particular sequence or event doesn't seem to work or fit. Discovering these problems at the pen-and-paper stage will save you a lot of heartache later on.

115

4

4
Notice that in these drawings the artist has indicated direction of movement using arrows. You can also draw in arrows and symbols to help you plan the camera moves between shots. Feel free to add any information that will help you later on.

ECONOMICAL MODELING 2

Try not to get so carried away with a particular object that you start adding in details that will never be seen. For example, the object's rear side never sees the camera, so you should not spend any time modeling it.

A similar rule applies to distant or insignificant objects in a scene. If a particular object is very distant or insignificant, then you can get away with making the model extremely simple—even just an impression or sketch will do. Much of the detail can be implied using textures, anyway.

116

1 | 2 | 3 | 4 | 5
This animation sequence is very simple (like the model). The camera moves from a long shot to a close-up on the front door. You could add some more detail to the door since it would be the prime focus of the shot, and the rest of the house can be well built and textured, too.

4

5

6

6
It's a very simple model, but no time at all was spent on the back of the house since it would never be seen. Planning a storyboard will also prevent you from having to recreate the back of the house if, in a later scene, it will be in shot. In that case, you'll save time by modeling the whole thing at the start.

DETAIL

3D graphics is all about making decisions. When you come to model an object, depending on its end use, you will decide how detailed you want it to be. Even simple models can end up being complex if they are going to be examined in detail, so how close the object will be to the camera in the final image will be a major factor in your model-making decisions. The other factor to consider is style, so if hyperrealism is your goal, then your models will need to be detailed. However, if you want a lo-fi look then you can use simple models.

In the following steps I've taken a familiar and deceptively simple object, a billiard cue, and tackled its modeling in three different ways. The modeling lesson is divided up into three detail sections—low detail, medium detail, and high detail.

118

2

1

1
Low detail
In the first example, a very simple model of the cue was made because it was going to be used in a computer game. A polygon cylinder Primitive was added to the scene, with eight sides and no divisions along its length. I also made sure it had caps.

2
If I wanted to be really picky, I could delete the eight triangles that composed each cap and replace them with a single eight-sided polygon. I was not that fussy, so I just carried on modeling. To create the cue, I selected the points that made up one of the ends of the cylinder and uniformly scaled them.

3
Once I got that far I could have decided that the cue was too short. Since the points were still selected, I could move them in the negative x direction to make the cue longer and skinnier.

4
And that's it finished. In the context of the other models, a billiard ball and table, the model is sufficient for its intended purpose.

1

120 **Medium detail.**
Next, a moderately
detailed model was
created, perhaps for
use in a realistic
scene, but not close
up. I began by
adding a Cylinder
Primitive again.

2
It's a parametric
Primitive, so I made
use of some of its
features, including
rounding, resolution

and its dimensions.
I activated the
rounding option
and set the size to
give it a nice edge.

3
Next the cylinder's
dimensions were
altered. If I just
scaled the cylinder,
rather than use its
parameters, the round
would also become

scaled in one direction
and therefore would
become lopsided. The
length was set to 4,000
units, the radius to 50
units, and the length
segments set to 1.

4
Next the parametric
cylinder was 'frozen'
into a simple polygon
object. It no longer
had any parameters,
but maintained the
shape that had been
set up. As in the low-
detail model, the end
points were selected
and scaled uniformly
in order to create
the pointed end.

6

6

The tip was added to the cue as a separate object to facilitate texturing later on. The end was rounded and the whole thing closely butted against the end of the cue. The ends were not overlapped, so that the rounds on the cue would still be visible, since they might catch some nice highlights in the final render.

5

A polygon cube was used as a cutting tool to remove a portion of the thick end of the cue, to create the detail you usually see on billiard cues. This was done with a Boolean subtraction operation.

8

7

7

Color and reflection image maps were created in Photoshop to make the material for the tip object. This is the reflection image used. Where the image is black the surface will not be reflective; where it is white (for the metallic part of the tip) it will be reflective.

8

Next the texture map for the tip was created in Photoshop and applied to the tip model.

9

Here is the finished render of the cue. It is moderately detailed and will look good in most situations, as long as there is not an extreme close-up shot.

9

1

High detail
For the super-high-resolution cue I began with the tip, since this is what will be seen in most detail. The very end of the tip was created from a cylinder with rounded edges, as before.

2
Because I knew I would be sculpting the model to add some irregularity, I needed to make sure that there were plenty of polygons when I came to freeze the procedural object. I increased the resolution to create a fine mesh.

3
Two more rounded cylinders were added to create a leather washer and the brass collar of the cue tip. Once again, these were set to have a high-mesh resolution.

122

5
The cylinder for the cue tip was sculpted using a Magnet tool. Other programs use similar tools (proportional, soft selection, etc.). The Magnet tool lets you pull on a mesh using a radius of influence—where you click is affected 100 percent, but the influence on surrounding points within the radius drops off smoothly. This means that you can sculpt polygon meshes like clay.

4
Before the procedurals were frozen into polygons, I thought it prudent to make duplicates, which could either be saved in a different file or just hidden. If I needed to go back and change something, such as the rounding radius or resolution, I could. If I was stuck with the polygon meshes I couldn't go back and change their basic shape as easily. Once safely duplicated, the remaining objects were then converted to polygons.

6
The leather washer and brass collar were also sculpted, but the collar was deformed using a smaller radius to create dents and dings.

7

Unlike the medium-resolution cue, this tip is in three sections, so it must be textured separately. The tip incorporated the technique of layering multiple textures and was actually created with procedural shaders rather than bitmaps. The first layer is a simple layer of noise, in both the color and bump channels of its material.

8

To simulate the effect of fuzz or chalk dust on the tip, a Fresnel shader was added to control the luminosity channel. This lightens the faces of the tip that are pointing away from the camera.

10

Finally, I made the chalk layer. This is another noise procedural that uses the alpha/transparency channel with a light blue color.

9

The next layer is the scuff layer. This is another noise procedural, but is used in the alpha channel of the texture (in most programs the transparency channel will work too). The color of the layer is black so that I could get the effect of wear and tear on the tip.

11

The other two sections were textured using the same technique of layering textures. Fresnel shaders are a big help when recreating materials at small scales, since they can suggest the fuzzy edges you see on small organic surfaces, such as fabric, suede, etc. A Fresnel shader was also used to control the reflection from the brass collar. Here is the finished cue tip, ready to be rendered up close.

12|13

In the final image, the scene is composed and lit as normal, but the camera is able to approach the cue for a really close shot.

THE IMPORTANCE OF EDGES

Edges are very important—not only the edges of each polygon, but the edges that define the form of an object. They set the limits of objects, their profiles, and separate areas of shading. Many modelers don't think about modeling the edges of an object because they are a direct result of the modeling process, so the modelers believe they don't have to create them manually. Real objects do not have infinitely sharp edges; they are blunt, rounded-off, or chamfered. This softening of edges makes your 3D objects look more realistic. Edges catch highlights (or darkness) to help separate adjoining faces with a definite line. Consider the following example.

1

1
Here is a simple 3D icon. It looks fine, but in places the edges don't separate the areas of similar shading too well, which results in the form being hidden in places.

2

3

3
Here is a close-up
of the beveled edge.
Notice how the bevel
catches highlights and
clearly separates the
front and sides of
the object.

2
Now look at this image.
See the difference?
A tiny bevel has been
added to the edges of
the extruded object.

ANIMATION 1

In 3D computer graphics, animation is the production of a sequence of images that shows an event that changes over time. It may be simply a ball bouncing, an army of robots fighting a pitched battle, a herd of dinosaurs romping across the Jurassic countryside, or anything else that can be imagined.

Each image represents a frame, the simplest whole division of time in the world of 3D animation. The term "frame" comes from film and broadcasting, where the "real-time" images you see on screen are merely single snapshots of time that are played one after another in sequence. They seem to merge into one continuous time stream because of two particular quirks of the human eye/brain system called "the persistence of vision" and "the phi phenomenon." Your brain retains a "memory" of an image for a few moments after you've experienced it, so that a staccato sequence of still images blends together to give the impression of smooth movement. The human brain is also quite good at interpolating missing information, especially from closely spaced events— filling in the blanks, as it were—to recreate what it expects it should be seeing.

The persistence of vision and the phi phenomenon are the reasons why simple devices such as the zoetrope succeed in creating moving images so easily.

In the world of film, each second in actual time is represented by 24 frames. So

1
A zoetrope works by rotating a sequence of images, which form an animated sequence when viewed. The machine works on the same principle as film and television, by producing a series of still images in quick succession.

1

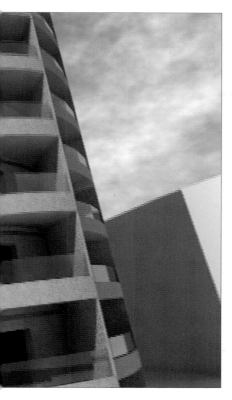

2
The two fields in the image are of two slightly different points in time in this animation. You can see the position of the tower is different in the two fields.

3
When motion is too quick to be captured by the camera shutter you get motion blur. This is a natural effect in both human visual systems and cameras. Motion blur in video systems often looks different to film blur because of the higher frame rate and the fact that the frames are split up into different time fields.

film is said to be "24 frames-per-second" or 24 fps. In broadcasting, there is more than one standard, depending upon which part of the world you live in. In Europe the broadcasting system is PAL, while in Japan, the United States, and Canada it is NTSC. In other parts of the world, including the former USSR and parts of Africa, it is SECAM. Aside from other technical variations in these standards that don't concern us here, broadcasting systems have different frame rates. PAL is 25 frames per second, NTSC is 30 fps, and SECAM is 25 fps.

To confuse things even more, the frame rates for these video standards are further split into fields, with each field containing half a frame. In fact, the frame is divided into alternating lines, so that one is set odd and the next even (1, 3, 5 , 7. . . and 2, 4, 6, 8, etc.). The important aspect of this splitting is that the fields represent two different slices of time, so video can really be thought of as 50 or 60 fields per second, rather than merely 25 or 30 fps. The result is that time is sampled more finely by video, and, therefore, motion is captured with greater resolution.

In film, the lower frame rate, combined with the technicalities of the way that an image is captured to film, results in something known as motion blur, a beneficial artifact that actually helps to smooth rapid motion by providing the impression of finer time sampling. Motion blur in film occurs when a fast-moving object changes its position while a single frame is being exposed. It's exactly the same as what happens when you move your head or arms during a long-exposure photograph.

129

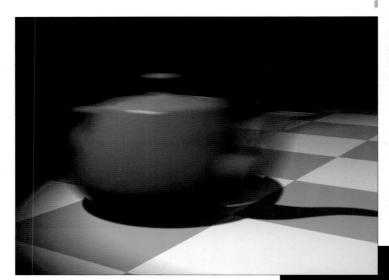

The human eye experiences a similar effect to the motion blur of film, which is partly why film motion blur looks so natural. Hold your hand up 1½ ft (0.5m) from your face with only your index finger extended. Now rapidly shake your hand from side to side (in the same plane as your palm) keeping your finger rigid. You should see motion blur as your finger moves quickly and, if you are observant, two stationary fingers at the points where your hand changes direction! Try it in front of a TV or monitor. You should see a collection of well-defined fingers silhouetted against the screen but no blur—the flickering of the CRT display creates a simulated "sampling" of the motion.

As a 3D animator, it is necessary to know on which standard the animation is going to be played so that the animation software can be set up for 24, 25, or 30 fps beforehand. You also need to know whether you will output the rendered images as frames or fields. Some 3D artists deliberately render at the film frame rate, then stretch the footage temporally in a compositing program to get more of a "film look." This is because there's more to the look of film than merely the frame rate, including grain or noise, contrast, and color balance.

If you render a 3D animation at 24 fps as if it were film footage, then don't expect to see any motion blur. The perfection of the virtual camera in computer animation software is such that this real-world aberration is eliminated. Motion blur has to be put back into a 3D scene, often with great effort (on the part of the computer's CPU). Motion blur needs to be calculated and

❚
With motion blur enabled, a moving object is rendered as a blur in the direction of motion. Vector motion blur does have limitations— notice that the teapot's shadow is not blurred.

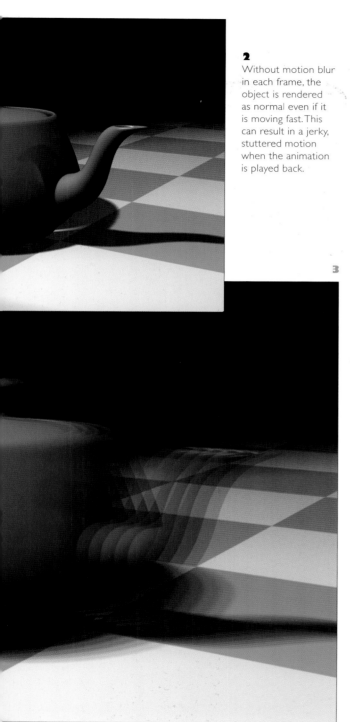

2
Without motion blur in each frame, the object is rendered as normal even if it is moving fast. This can result in a jerky, stuttered motion when the animation is played back.

3

added back into the final render as an additional process, which means that rendering realistic animations requires more computing power than a still image. It was only thanks to motion-blur simulation that the 3D dinosaurs in *Jurassic Park* made it to celluloid. Any 3D animation without motion blur will not blend well with traditionally shot footage, unless there is very little movement.

So if you are animating for broadcasting or film, motion blur is going to be an important consideration. In 3D there are three types of motion blur—2D, 3D, and multiframe. 3D motion blur uses sophisticated techniques to calculate highly accurate motion blur in three dimensions, but this is very time-consuming. An alternative is 2D motion blur, which uses a very simple technique for calculating motion-blur effects. For every element in the scene, the motion vector is calculated with respect to the viewing plane. This means that the movement of every element across the screen is analyzed and a motion-vector amplitude is calculated. Because only 2D vectors are calculated, the process is much quicker, though not quite as accurate as the 3D technique. Nevertheless, the results of motion-vector motion blur are, nine times out of ten, indistinguishable from real footage to the average viewer.

Because of the greater time sampling of video, you may not need software to calculate motion blur with video footage. Even with video, there are times when a fast-moving object will require motion blur or you may suffer staccato, strobing animations.

3
With multiframe motion blur, subframes are rendered of the scene or object and then blended together to give the final frame. This can be more accurate when lots of subframes are rendered, but is very expensive computationally. This is because for each frame, five or more frames are actually rendered. This image uses five-frame multiframe motion blur, and you can clearly see each subframe in the blur, though the shadow is now blurred, too. The image took five times longer to render than the previous image.

131

KEYFRAME ANIMATION

In 3D, animation is achieved using a process called keyframing. This is a technique that derives its name from traditional 2D cel animation, where a key artist would block out the main poses of an animated character, letting assistant animators fill the frames in between. The keyframes were therefore the frames that were drawn by the key animator. In 3D animation you are the key animator and the computer is your assistant, ready to fill in the frames between the keyframes you set.

In the case of a simple animation, such as a ball rolling across the floor, you begin by setting a keyframe that records the starting position of the ball at frame 1. Then you move to the final frame of the animation, say, frame 50, and move the ball 100 units in x and record another keyframe. The software interpolates between these keys to produce values for the ball's position at each frame between 1 and 50.The result is that the ball moves across the screen when you play the animation. A quick bit of simple math will also tell you what values you use for the final rotation of the ball, given the 100 units it has traveled. The ball will then roll as it moves (without appearing to slide) across the screen.

The interpolation of keyframes, often known as "tweening," is very important. A linear interpolation produces an

1
The function curve shows how animation data changes over time. The vertical scale is the animation data value, and the horizontal scale is time.

2
An ease-in, ease-out function curve looks like a gentle, slanting S-shape.

132

animation with no acceleration. In the case of the rolling ball, it would appear to start rolling immediately, roll at a constant velocity, and then stop dead. This is not very natural and is contrary to physical laws! What you'd expect to see is the ball smoothly accelerate from rest, reach a constant velocity, then decelerate until it comes to rest again. In order to get this effect you must tell the software to handle the keyframe interpolation differently. Because this smoothly accelerating motion is very common in animation, the interpolation is given a name, "ease-in, ease-out." Some software lets you choose the interpolation type from a list of presets, but this is very limiting. The better 3D software lets you create arbitrary interpolation using function curves.

133

3
Linear interpolation is represented by a straight line between keyframes.

Function curves are graphical representations that demonstrate the way the animation data is changing over time, and they are drawn using a simple curve on a graph. An ease-in, ease-out curve would look like a slanting S-shape, while linear interpolation would be seen as a straight line.

A good function-curve editor will let you modify the shape of the curve using tangent handles, like a Bézier curve in a drawing program. This gives you excellent control over the curve shape, without having to add extra keyframes. Another way to control the curves is to use TCB controls (Tension, Continuity and Bias), which are three values that a keyframe can have that modifies the shape of the incoming and outgoing curve. Other interpolation methods include Cubic, which is not as controllable but provides a useful, smooth interpolation for some situations.

The best 3D computer software will allow you to mix these interpolation methods on the same function curve, which will give you the best control over timing that you could expect.

4

Here is the function-curve editor in Lightwave. It lets you mix different interpolation types on the same curve, so some keyframes use linear interpolation, others Bézier; some Hermite, and others TCB.

5

Breakdowns are special keys that keep their relative distance between their neighboring keys. Here, in Maya, the breakdown lies between two Bézier keys.

6

By moving just the last keyframe backward a few frames, the breakdown moves, too, maintaining its relationship between the two keys. This is very useful because you can use it to scale a segment of an animation without having to use a special tool or move each keyframe manually.

135

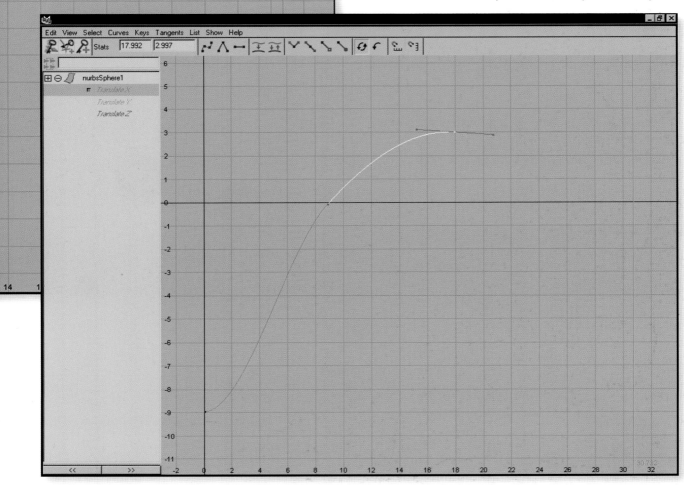

6

ANIMATING JOINTED HIERARCHIES

hough even intermediate character animation is beyond the scope of this book (I recommend the highly regarded *Character Animation* by George Maestri if you want to explore the nuances of animating 3D characters), some basic techniques will be discussed. Some of the common methods used to animate digital characters will also be demonstrated.

A simple 3D character might be composed of a series of hierarchically linked objects, such as a head, torso, shoulder, forearm, hand, and fingers. Each one is a separate object with its own carefully placed pivot point (Local axis).

When animating a character by rotating each object in turn in a hierarchy, you are carrying out what is known as Forward Kinematics (FK). When you move your arm in order to pick something up, you don't think about first moving your shoulder joint, then your forearm and then your hand; you just reach with your hand. In the computer, this type of motion can also be achieved by using Inverse Kinematics (IK). With an IK hierarchy, you grab the end object to rotate the objects all at once further up the hierarchy.

Many 3D animators prefer to use FK for the arms of a character, but IK for the legs. They use FK for the arms because the legs usually have to stay planted on the floor. IK can be used for the arms when the character is holding onto something, for example, if it is climbing a ladder. A 3D system that lets you use both FK and IK at the same time is advantageous, but in many 3D programs IK and FK are mutually exclusive.

136

2
If you try to rotate the pieces of the arm to animate it, the arm will come apart.

1
In a hierarchical arrangement of objects that are part of a 3D character, each object's Local axes need to be properly positioned. Here is an arm in which each object's axes remain in their default positions.

3
By moving each
object's axes near
the object that is its
parent, rotating the
objects creates the
correct result.

137

4

4
This arm has been set
up to use IK and also
feature a few extra
objects in the hierarchy,
though there are still
three joints. With IK,
you usually need to
specify where the start
and end points of the
IK chain are. The start
is the shoulder, but the
end, in this case, is a
Null object (an object
that has no
geometry)z, which has
made a child of the
hand. All you need to
do to bend the arm is
to move the Null.

ANIMATING SINGLE-SKIN CHARACTERS 1

So far, we've seen examples for a character composed of separate objects linked into a hierarchy. Such a model is useful but not very realistic. To create a believable monster, human, dog, etc., you'll probably create the model using a single mesh of polygons or stitched NURBS surfaces. Since the model is a single object without a hierarchy, you need to create a skeleton so that the joints can be added back into the model.

There are two types of skeletons, one constructed of joints and one of bones. Joints and bones sound similar, but they work slightly differently and some programs favor one over the other. Their main purpose is to define a structure within the model that can be bent and moved like a hierarchical model. The resulting single-skin model is then linked to the skeleton in such a way that it deforms when the skeleton limbs are rotated.

It's the way the linking is done that makes joints and bones different. With a bone, all the points on a linked skin model within a certain radius are affected by it. If you move the bone, then the points move with it. When two bones are linked to a skin model they are in competition for control over the points, so the points closest to each bone are "captured" by it and move

with that bone. Close to where two bones are connected (a limb joint), the points make a smooth transition from being controlled by one bone to the other, and a few points are controlled by both at once. The result is that rotating one bone causes the skin to deform with the rotating bone in a natural way.

In a complex bone hierarchy, all of the bones are in competition for all of the points in a mesh. Usually, this results in the correct points being affected, but it can

1
Here is a simple flat plane with one bone linked to it. The bone is displayed as a toothpick-like object in the 3D view.

2
When the bone is rotated, the entire plane moves with it because the points are fully influenced by the single bone.

138

cause problems such as arm bones affecting the chest, etc. Animators will usually add special anchor bones to the model to hold in place parts of the model that they don't want to deform, such as the head and chest or perhaps equipment that the character is wearing.

In order to minimize this extra setup, you often see character models that are constructed in an "X" stance, with their arms outstretched and level with their shoulders, and with their legs and fingers apart. This helps to keep extremities separated from other parts of the body so that, when boned, the deforming effects of the bones are restricted to those parts of the body they are meant to affect.

3

When two bones are linked in a hierarchy to the plane, something quite different occurs. Rotating one of the bones deforms the plane, since some of the points are captured by one bone while the rest are captured by the other bones.

ANIMATING SINGLE-SKIN CHARACTERS 2

2

With skeletal joints, points are assigned to bones directly, no matter what distance they are from the joint. In other words, a single mesh with one joint would not necessarily have all its points captured. In a hierarchical setup, the joints have points allocated to them, then, close to the area that will be deformed the points must be "weighted" between each pair of joints. Some programs link the joints in a skeleton without weighting the points between each pair of joints, resulting in a rigid binding; points belong to either one joint or another. When you rotate a joint in this type of setup the mesh will not deform smoothly, so a complex series of special devices, called lattices, is used to create smooth deformations.

1

persp

1
A single-skin character is, as its name implies, constructed from a single mesh of polygons or a single parametric surface. This polygon velociraptor has had a jointed skeleton built inside it, to which it will later be bound. The process of binding, or skinning as it is sometimes known, maps the mesh vertices to particular joints in the skeleton based on a distance.

2
In the case of joints, points are linked to individual joints by the process of binding. In this example colors are used to show which points are bound to which joints.

3
Weighted, or smooth, binding, results in smooth joint deformations because the points are mapped to joint pairs using a weighting value. Unlike bones, joints only affect specific points, not the whole model. In Maya, the weights can be visualized as grayscale values displayed on the mesh in OpenGL. A brush can then be used to paint or smooth the weighting.

141

3

ANIMATION GUIDELINES

One of the great advantages of 3D computer graphics is the total freedom you can have with animation. Almost everything can be animated, but just because you can animate something doesn't always mean that you should. A prime example of this is the camera. It's very easy to animate a 3D virtual camera. There's no need for a cameraman and there are no tripods or dollies to lug around and set up. If you want to do a crane shot, you don't need to rent the equipment, there's no worry about the weather being unsuitable, and you don't have someone to tell you, "You can't do that." Because 3D cameras can move through objects, or move in ways that are impossible to recreate with traditional photography, it's very easy for an inexperienced animator to get carried away.

Wild camera moves are distracting, and sometimes even uncomfortable, to watch. A demo reel full of animations where half of the action is due to the camera moving all over the place doesn't look professional.

The best way to learn about camera techniques is to watch some movies or TV programs and make notes. Most of the time the camera is hardly moving, and variation is provided by editing between different shots instead of moving the camera itself.

142

1
A 3D virtual camera enables you to move easily through shots, as the next four images show. You can show a full shot of the model, for example.

2
Then move in on a medium shot of the model.

3
A close-up. of the model.

If the camera does need to move, then gentle, considered movements are recommended. Generally, camera moves should not draw attention to themselves—except if you want to create a special effect. For example, a good technique for creating a camera effect is to shake two camera position channels using a succession of randomly generated keyframes to simulate the effect of a shockwave (from an explosion, for example) hitting the camera. Another similar technique is

achieved to generate POV (point of view) shots. Some randomization of the keyframe data can be used to create handheld camera effects, or to simulate a bumpy road surface if the POV is from a person riding in a car.

Toy Story is a good movie to watch for tips on many aspects of 3D animation. The camera work is very controlled, but creative, too. However, it is a good idea to get a book on cinematic photography techniques for more detailed descriptions of 3D animation techniques.

143

4
And, finally, an extreme close-up.

5
A long shot is used to establish the location in which a following shot takes place.

…</>

2

1

When cutting between two characters in conversation, you must always be careful to observe the line of sight when placing the camera. The line of sight is an imaginary plane between the two characters. The camera must always be on one side of the line of sight in such a situation.

144

2

If the camera passes the line of sight, it will appear that one of the characters is facing the wrong way and you'll confuse the viewer.

3 | 4 | 5
When cutting between close-ups, if the camera crosses the line of sight, you get this.

6 | 7 | 8
If the camera remains on the same side of the plane there is no confusion, and both characters appear to be talking to each other.

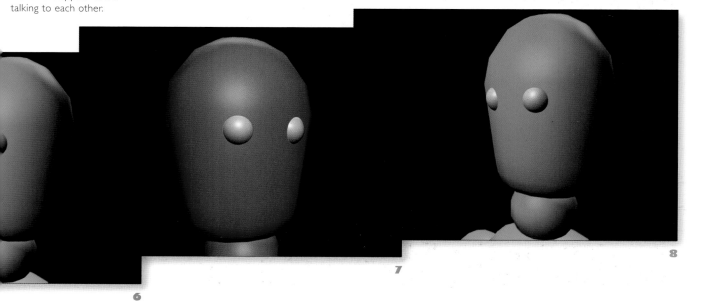

UV TEXTURE MAPPING 1

Projections are one way in which to apply textures to objects, but there is also another method of applying textures—UV texture mapping. Projection mapping is used because the 3D software doesn't have any understanding of the structure of the surface. In the case of NURBS models, however, the structure of the surface is well known. A NURBS surface is constructed of curves that run in two directions, perpendicular to each other. Even if the NURBS surface happens to be wildly convoluted, this surface structure is always maintained. In the same way as the x and y coordinates of 3D space, locations on a NURBS surface can also be described in terms of coordinates. These coordinates are called "U" and "V" and represent the opposing directions that the curves follow.

▌
A flat NURBS plane would have U along one direction and V along the other. The corner that has both U and V values of 0 is the origin of the surface, written 0,0. In the opposite corner, the UV values are 1,1. A point anywhere on the surface can be located by finding its U and V coordinate values.

2
Here is a simple texture applied using UV mapping to a fingerlike object.

3
Because the texture is effectively locked to the UV coordinates, you can deform the object and have the texture deform with it. In fact, as far as the texture is concerned, the UV coordinates of the surface are not deforming at all.

With UV mapping, as it is called, everything basically boils down to a simple flat projection, no matter what the actual shape of the surface is. Every NURBS surface in UV coordinate space looks like a flat plane, and it is extremely easy to map a flat plane.

The other property of UV texture mapping is that it is possible to stick the texture to the surface. The texture is pinned down, as it were, at the NURBS CVs so that as the object is deformed, the texture is deformed along with it.

3

UV TEXTURE MAPPING 2

The unique feature of UV textures is that the UV points can be moved in relation to the texture image. This has the effect of letting us distort the texture image so that it more accurately fits the object on which it is being mapped.

In some systems this UV mapping process can be taken a step further by allowing the artist to paint the texture map directly on the object, using the UV coordinates as a guide. This has obvious benefits, since it takes the guesswork out of placing details in textures.

1

Here is an image of the area around an eye being mapped using default UV coordinates. As you can see, it doesn't quite fit.

2

You can view the UV points of the object as a flat 2D plane and place the image underneath. This lets you see exactly how the UV points (or, rather, the surface points with known UV coordinates) lie in relation to the texture image.

3

By moving the UVs you can line them up with features in the face image, thus making the image stretch to fit the geometry in the 3D view. The result is a perfectly mapped object.

GENERATING UVS FOR POLYGON OBJECTS

Nurbs surfaces are not the only geometry type that can utilize UV coordinates. As we have seen, there's no way for the software to work out the UV coordinates of an arbitrary polygon mesh since there may not be a well-defined U and V direction. However, you can force the UVs onto a mesh that has already had a projection applied to it. Thus, you effectively "bake" the UVs into a polygon mesh based on an initial projection method, be it planar, cylindrical, spherical, etc.

1
A polygon surface has no UV information by default, which is why you have to use projected textures.

2
Once the projection is applied, you may have the option (depending on the software) to bake the texture coordinates into the polygon points based on the projection.

3
This lets you use the same UV editing tools on polygon objects as for NURBS, enabling you to adjust the texture to make it fit the object better.

4

Here is one of the models that ships with Softimage XSI. The color texture for the robot is a single image map, with each section positioned to make maximum use of space in the image file. Features that are duplicated, such as each side of the face, legs, and arms, are only painted once in the map. By overlapping UVs that share a common part of the image, the details can be duplicated in different parts of the model. This is a good way to save time. If you have repeating details, you can paint just one iteration of the detail and make it repeat by overlapping the UVs in the 3D program. Many programs let you cut and paste large sections of UVs to speed up the process.

You can think of the initial projection as a starting point. Once the texture coordinates have been baked into the polygon surface, it can be unwrapped (or, rather, the projection is unwrapped, taking the polygons with it) and viewed as a flat plane. You can then begin moving the UV points so that the texture is more accurately positioned on the mesh.

With UV textures, you have the option to put all of your bitmap textures in a single image file for each channel. The position of any given surface-texture detail in the image is not important, so the texture can be optimized without wasting much space.

3D ON THE WEB

One of the emerging uses of 3D graphics is on the Web. It is inevitable, really, because 3D is the natural extension of the traditional 2D imagery that is so prevalent in today's Web content.

There are hurdles to overcome when it comes to delivering 3D content on the Web, though. The initial difficulty arises from the amount of data that goes into describing a 3D scene or object. When producing 3D work locally on your own computer, the size of the files you produce is not too much of a concern, especially with today's large-capacity hard drives, which are usually tens of gigabytes as a standard. If you had to transmit that data to someone else via the Internet using a 56k modem, however, the receiver would have a long wait.

What is needed is some way to reduce the information that is transmitted without degrading the 3D information too much. It's the same compromise that is faced by 2D designers who are optimizing images for the Web.

There are many companies working on their own custom schemes for producing this sort of 3D data compression, each hoping to become the standard. Flash is one example. It is more or less the standard for delivering rich 2D animated content with minimal data rates, so a 3D Web standard version would provide a universal solution that every browser and every 3D program would support.

The delivery of 3D content on the Internet falls into two broad categories, streaming and nonstreaming solutions. Nonstreaming solutions have been around for a while and rely on simple compression of the 3D data and texture to minimize transfer times. Technologies such as VRML and QuickDraw 3D are nonstreaming, which means that the entire 3D data must be downloaded before it can be displayed. With 3D content of any detail this means a long wait before the viewer sees the 3D object or scene in their Web browser—long enough for them to get impatient and go elsewhere.

Apple's QuickDraw 3D technology was pushed as a standard for interactive 3D graphics such as QuickTime and has become a standard for movie playback. Apple has since dropped support of QuickDraw in favor of OpenGL.

Streaming 3D incrementally delivers the data, which is reconstructed as and when the information is received. The model may be displayed almost immediately in a very rough, low-resolution form, but then, as more data is downloaded, the model becomes more detailed. This is obviously a superior, more elegant solution than the nonstreaming alternatives, and shows why most of the research effort in this field is in streaming 3D content. Streaming 3D lets you see the 3D model in stages and allows you to interact with it while it is downloading.

In both cases, the 3D data is sent raw and is reconstructed at the viewer's browser, usually with the help of a plug-in. The 3D object or scene is then rendered directly in the Web browser on the fly, so that the viewer can interact with the 3D object, rotating or zooming in on it. In this way, 3D content can be seamlessly integrated into Web pages without the need for a stand-alone application for viewing.

At the moment, there are numerous offerings, and this chapter gives you a taste of them.

2
QuickDraw 3D can be used to produce interactive 3D such as this roller-coaster-ride game.

VRML

Virtual Reality Markup Language, or VRML, is a non-streaming format touted by the nonprofit organization the Web|3D Consortium as the Internet standard for delivering interactive 3D content over the Web. It's now, in reality, a dinosaur that never actually delivered a truly interactive, rich 3D experience, due to the clumsiness of the delivery method.

The Web|3D Consortium is currently putting forward a new standard X3D to replace VRML, but it is likely to be usurped by companies researching streaming 3D content delivery. In the same way, Macromedia's Flash became the de facto standard, thanks to massive publicity by the company, despite other "official" standards already put in place.

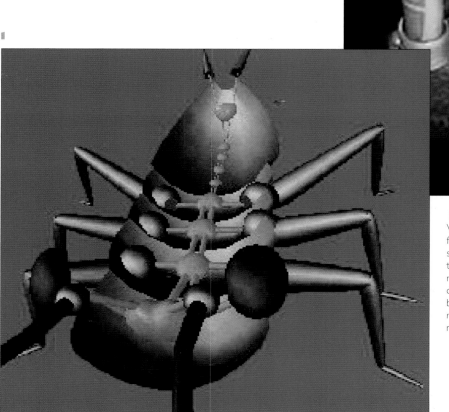

1

1
VRML is often used for interactive structures, such as this biological 3D representation of a cricket. The body can be removed to reveal the insect's nervous system.

2
VRML has been a successful system for Web 3D, and the file format is supported by most 3D programs. However, it requires a full download of the 3D data before displaying in the destination browser, so it's a clumsy and slow way to create 3D worlds online. Don't expect anything as exciting or impressive as this image in your browser.

157

3

3
Though people are finding new and (probably) exciting uses for 3D graphics on the Web, it's obvious application is for creating 3D environments. VRML has been used for games and chat room "worlds" such as this.

VIEWPOINT

Viewpoint was bought by MetaCreations, the company that was originally responsible for creating Photoshop plug-ins such as KPT, and 3D programs like Bryce and Poser. It subsequently divested itself of its graphics division to concentrate on interactive 3D for marketing, based around its Metastream technology. After buying Viewpoint and absorbing its vast libraries of 3D models, it dropped the MetaCreations moniker in favor of Viewpoint.

Viewpoint also licenses its streaming technology to other companies. Adobe, for example, has recently licensed it to create its own interactive and streaming 3D authoring environment, called Atmospheres. Based on the Viewpoint technology, it allows designers to create engaging 3D Web sites with the typical Adobe ease of use.

There are a number of programs that can export to the Viewpoint streaming format (previously called Metastream), including Poser 4 with Plus Pack, Cinema 4D XL, and 3D Studio Max.

1 | 2 | 3

The Viewpoint 3D format, previously called Metastream, delivers 3D models using streaming technology via the Viewpoint Media Player, the free browser plug-in required to view and interact with the 3D objects. At the time of writing, it seems the best choice in terms of speed and quality. This 3D model of a VW Beetle is viewed in a browser using Viewpoint 3D. It gives you the option to view the Beetle from different angles and to change the color as well.

158

4
An example site utilizing Viewpoint streaming 3D to sell jewelry. Users visiting the site to view the wares can modify the gemstone colors by clicking on a color swatch. The gems are instantaneously rerendered in the new color.

5
A complete version of Atmosphere was unavailable at the time of writing, but it is expected to be a full 3D authoring tool based on Viewpoint's Metastream technology. Examples of sites posted on Adobe's Web site look promising, though.

CULT3D

Cycore Computers offers up Cult3D, another potential streaming standard that is vying for dominance. Cult3D is a program that has similar streaming capabilities to Metastream (*see pages 158–59*), although it does not seem to have secured the backing that Viewpoint has managed to acquire.

Graphics home
Pick of the day
Advisory
History
Services
Team
Technical
Topics
MIR Space Station 3D
MIR Interactive 3D
Feedback

You will need the CULT3D plugin (1.2mb) to view the MIR graphics

DRAG ON OBJECTS WITH YOUR MOUSE

Animated graphic sequence courtesy Cult3d.com

Legal | Copyright | Privacy |

REUTERS

1
Like Viewpoint, Cult3D requires a free viewer plug-in for your Web browser.

2
You can interact with the streaming 3D model in real time, rotating or zooming in on it.

Graphics home
Pick of the day
Advisory
History
Services
Team
Technical

You will need the (

Station 3D

ctive 3D

DRAG

Animated

Legal | Copyright | Privacy |

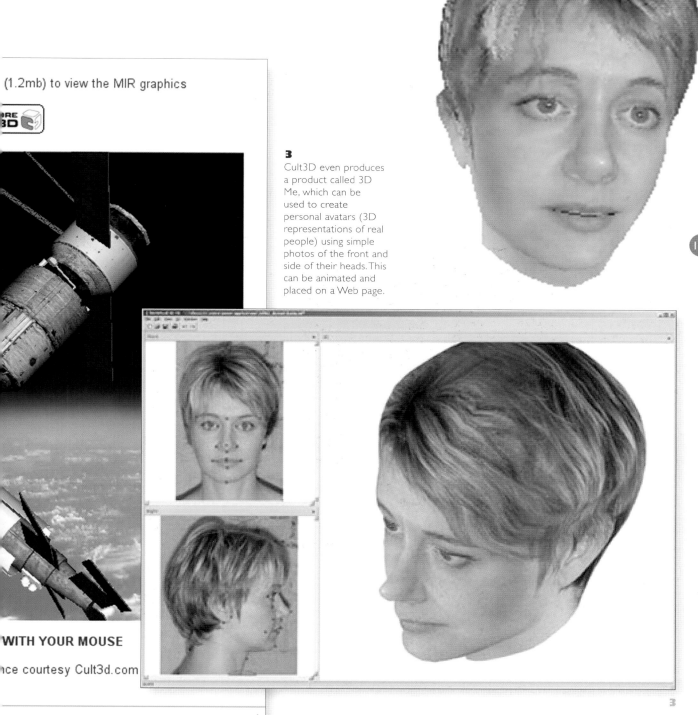

(1.2mb) to view the MIR graphics

3
Cult3D even produces a product called 3D Me, which can be used to create personal avatars (3D representations of real people) using simple photos of the front and side of their heads. This can be animated and placed on a Web page.

161

WITH YOUR MOUSE

ice courtesy Cult3d.com

CRYONETWORKS

Cryonetworks is a French company that has produced an entire language for delivering 3D multimedia sites capable of replacing HTML-based Web browsers and streaming media viewers. The language is SCOL; it provides a complete multimedia authoring framework that can incorporate 3D graphics, sound, QuickTime movies, chat rooms, HTML, and Java, and it can also be used to create multiuser virtual environments.

Though the meat and potatoes of this interactive 3D experience is displayed using special software, the SCOL Voy@ger, access to the sites can be broadcast using traditional browsers, which then open the SCOL Voy@ger application when you enter the site proper.

The downside to SCOL is that it is totally proprietary, needing unique software and hosting requirements, so it is not widely accepted. However, it does show that there are alternatives to the Web-browser-plug-in approach that has been taken by the majority of developers.

162

2

character generation.

ch
na

Straight out
the scientis
everything
almost ever
from ge
astronomy r
to electr
eclecticisr
positive f
advance
inventions
mankind. Ne
isn't naive

1

This is the Cryopolis site (**www.cryopolis.com**), which has been accessed using the SCOL Voy@ger from Cryonetworks. It's a multiuser 3D environment, complete with sound and chat. You can navigate the site by wandering around the 3D scenery, enter buildings, and meet other users.

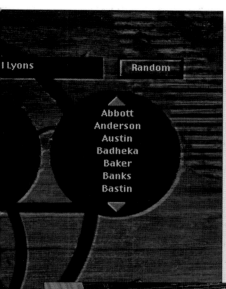

2 | 3

Another SCOL site is Fog (**www.fogmysteries.com**), an online adventure/ whodunit game in which you are a detective trying to solve a mystery. You can choose a character and enter the site as a fully animated 3D character. The graphics are comparable to a simple console game, but it is made more interesting because of the interactivity and multiplayer nature.

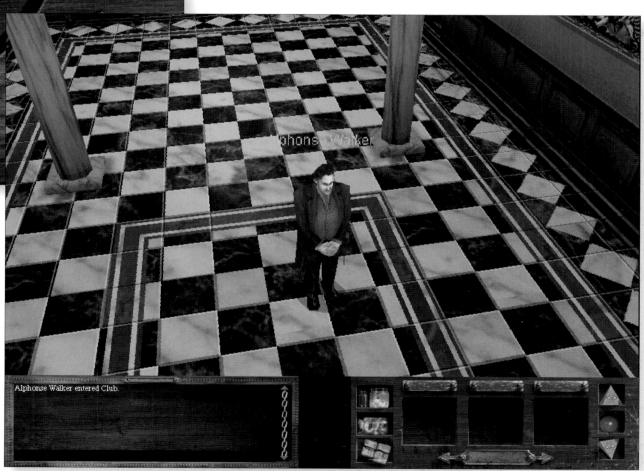

3

HYPERCOSM

Hypercosm gears its 3D system for the "eCRM" market, or online customer relations. It's also a useful system for designing online tutorials, instructions for equipment, and manuals for assembly and installation. Other uses include online virtual galleries and 3D representations of complex analytical data.

The interactive demo for a Hewlett-Packard printer uses the Hypercosm Netscape plug-in to display the 3D object in real time and provide animated instructions.

3D Web content is a useful way to provide instant training and instructional content and has many different uses. An animated set of instructions in 3D for assembling a piece of equipment (or furniture), as long as it has been well designed, could be more useful than the exploded diagrams we have been used to.

164

2

If tray is not already set to desired paper size, snap guides into place to match width of paper.

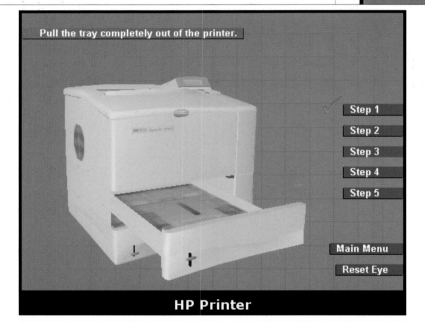

Pull the tray completely out of the printer.

Step 1
Step 2
Step 3
Step 4
Step 5

Main Menu
Reset Eye

HP Printer

HP Printer

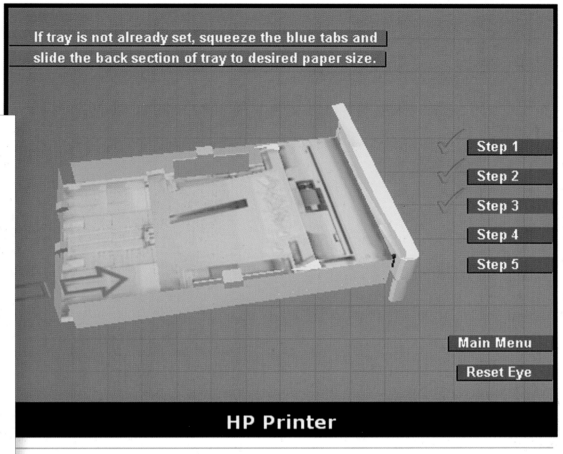

If tray is not already set, squeeze the blue tabs and
slide the back section of tray to desired paper size.

Step 1

Step 2

Step 3

Step 4

Step 5

Main Menu

Reset Eye

HP Printer

Step 1

Step 2

Step 3

Step 4

Step 5

Main Menu

Reset Eye

P, its marks, products, logos, or brands are property of the hewlett-packard company.

copyright © 2000 Hypercosm, Inc. | Showcase | Back

d company.

165

1 | 2 | 3
This is an interactive
demo for a Hewlett-
Packard printer. It
uses the Hypercosm
Netscape plug-in to
display the 3D object
in real time, and also
provides animated
instructions.

SUN AND JAVA 3D

Sun is the company that developed the platform-independent Java programing language. Java is a platform-independent environment in which programs written in the Java language can run irrespective of the machine they are running on. Java implements a "virtual machine" that is like a software ideal of a computer, isolating the program and any calls it makes to hardware from the actual machine the environment is running on.

Sun has now also introduced an extension to the Applicatin Programing Interface (API), called Java 3D, which provides interactive 3D for Java. It is currently only available for Windows and Unix systems, but a Mac version is expected soon. The good thing about the Java 3D program is that you can download and display interactive 3D content from any Java-enabled browser without the need to first download a plug-in.

This 3D option is intriguing and elegant because it is totally independent of the platform and browser. That means there's no need to download and install a new plug-in each time the format is upgraded. How many times have you had to do that with Flash?

So, when it comes to delivering 3D content on the Internet, there are a number of excellent offerings, and I've discussed examples of just a few of them in this chapter. It's only a matter of time until we find out which will become the standard and it's likely to be the solution that offers the richest experience and the speediest downloads that shines through.

166

2

Intel® Pentium®II Xeon™ Processor

- **Cartridge**
  - Connector
  - Thermal plate
  - Heat sink
- **Substrate**
- **CPU core**

Sound On
Narration On

Developed by Intel, the Single Edge Contact (S.E.C...
high-volume availability, improved handling protect...
common form factor for future Pentium(R) II Xeon(TM) processors.

Intel® Pentium®II X

- **Cartridge**
- ▶**Substrate**
  - Level 2 cache
  - SMBus
  - Thermal sensor
  - Scratch EEPROM
  - PIROM
- **CPU core**

Sound On
Narration On

The CPU
interface
processo

3

Intel® Pentium®II Xeon™ Processor | tour

- **Cartridge**

- **Substrate**

▶ **CPU core**

　Level 1 cache
　Thermal diode
　450/400 MHz cor
　　speeds

Processo

▪ **Sound On**
▪ **Narration On**

The Pentium(R) II Xeon(TM) processor's 450 MHz or 400 MHz core speeds work in tandem with the L2 cache. This makes an unprecedented amount of data available for processing.

167

1 | 2 | 3
This site uses Java 3D to create the interactive tour of the Intel Pentium processor. Though, like the processor, Java 3D is slightly slower than the other streaming 3D alternatives, there is no plug-in to install, so the site can be accessed immediately. This site uses the SpaceCrafter pure Java Rendering engine by InWorld VR Inc.

he and the new System Management bus
nounted directly to the substrate inside the
trid ge.

OTHER OPTIONS: PRERENDERED 3D SCENES

There are alternatives to sending the actual 3D data to a viewer's browser. With Flash, you can prerender the images and convert them into Flash vector data, much more efficient and faster than sending compressed bitmaps. Some 3D programs let you render directly to Flash format, which is a big plus and saves a conversion step.

The other way is with good old GIF animation. It's clunky and not terribly efficient, but, for many uses, a GIF animation may suffice. However, there are limitations with the prerendered option. There is little or no interactivity, or, if there is, it has to be worked out in advance. With Flash, there are no complex materials for objects, since it works best when areas of flat color are used. A cartoon 3D look will usually be the result, with material details such as reflection, transparency, and bumps removed; and graduated shading will be reduced to three or fewer flat areas of color. Nevertheless, you

over website

® Registered trade i

3
GIF animation can be created by rendering a normal animated image sequence from your 3D program, such as this animation of the construction of an Intel processor.

2
Flash is based on vectors rather than bitmaps, so only the information required to create the images is set, rather than the images themselves.

1
Cartoon-look images are suited to Flash-based animation because they are made of areas of flat color. You could model characters like this in 3D for Flash output.

still have the power of perspective, movement, color, and scale to play with, which can be put to use with great effect by using Flash and a 3D program.

The precise shape and scope of 3D graphics on the Internet is uncertain, but it is inevitable that 3D graphics will become a major player in Web marketing, gaming, and communication. Precisely what form the next generation of 3D Web graphics will take and how it will be delivered remains a subject of speculation, but the fervor with which companies are currently developing 3D Web technology indicates that the picture will clarify sooner rather than later.

ARCHITECTURE

3D graphics are ideal for visualizing architectural designs. Instead of building scale models out of foamboard and balsa wood, a 3D model can be generated from architectural plans using a computer.

With realistic lighting, a 3D render can help show how light in a building will look. Simulations can be carried out to show how lighting will change throughout the year, and, by using radiosity techniques, accurate renderings of buildings and lighting can be achieved.

2
3D rendering aids the process of visualizing interior spaces. Radiosity and raytracing can help show how a space will look when actually built. (Image © Hammel, Green and Abrahamson, Inc.)

3
3D rendering can help architects to visualize how the chosen building materials will look in the final building. (Image © Michael D. Abbott/ Vantage Graphics & Design Ltd.)

172

1
Architectural models can be created from building plans. The models can then be textured and lit for final rendering. (Image © Hammel, Green and Abrahamson, Inc.)

4
Both on a large and
a small scale, a 3D
model can communicate
the feel of a space
much more readily to
a client. (Image © Rob
Herrmann Design.)

5
This huge model
shows how easy it is
to get an overview of
a very large space
using a 3D program.
(Image © Entolo.)

ARTISTIC/ILLUSTRATION

3D graphics are used by digital artists to create illustrations for print and the Web. With a 3D program, there are no limits to what can be achieved, and often artists will choose not to go for the photo-real look when creating 3D illustrations. Thankfully, 3D programs allow you to create hyperrealistic images just as well as photoreal ones.

3

This image, rendered in ElectricImage, is a good example of extreme hyperreal surfaces. The metal in the image looks particularly lush and rich. (Image © Paul Sherstobitoff.)

3

1

1

This illustration by the author was created for *MacUser* magazine. The petals on the flower were textured in order to enhance their edges and provide a stylized look to the image.

2

This simple and tranquil scene makes good use of scene fog effects. (Image © William Green.)

2

4
An image produced for *Computer Arts* magazine by the author. Rounded edges in the model help to define the shapes by catching specular highlights.

5
This image, another created for *Computer Arts* magazine by the author, uses luminance maps for most of the illumination. The only real lights are the four spotlights and an uplight.

175

4

5

PHOTO-REALISM

One of the main uses for 3D graphics is creating images that attempt to look like the real thing. Every artist has his or her own trick for achieving a photorealisitc look, but lighting is the key ingredient. Though none of the images below and right uses radiosity, they all approach realism in varying degrees.

Most mid- to high-range software packages can be used for photo-real rendering, though some are easier to use than others. Cheaper 3D programs are more limiting.

3
Simple everyday objects can be used for rendering studies. This image, created for *Computer Arts* magazine by the author, demonstrates that modeling detail can also play a big part.

1
Exterior scenes in bright sunlight tend to have hard shadows and lots of contrast. This temple image demonstrates this well. (Image © Eric Hanson.)

2
Intricate texture details can work wonders. This incredible image has excellent texturing on the ants and the vegetation. (Image © Cristobal Vila, Eterea Animation Studios.)

3

2

4
Despite not being rendered using radiosity, this image shows the effect of exterior lighting on an overcast day. The soft, diffuse shadows and lighting are created using a Lightwave plug-in called, appropriately, Overcaster. (Image © AKMP-Program Oy 2001.)

5
Creating realistic gold and metal can be a tricky business. If you want to render a reflective metallic object in isolation, you'll need to add an environment map or there will be nothing to reflect. (Image © Cristobal Vila, Eterea Animation Studios.)

ETEREA. Cristóbal Vila. 2000

5

REAL-TIME 3D

For real-time use, you need to make special considerations for the modeling and texturing. For games and any interactive 3D use, models need to be "light." In other words, they must be made up of as few polygons as possible. The heavier the model, the longer it will take a games console or computer to display it, impacting interactivity.

Game modeling requires a special skill, where economy is king. All the models on this page are created using only a handful of polygons; clever texturing, then, makes up for what is missing.

2

2
Clever texturing helps to make low-resolution models more believable. The spinning rotors on these helicopters are made to look like blurred rotorblades by using a texture map. (Image © Geoff Holman.)

1
A typical game model, this tank is made using only a small number of polygons. The less work a console or computer does trying to draw the model, the faster the game will run. (Image © Geoff Holman.)

1

3

3
Bump mapping plays an important role in low-resolution modeling (as in all types of 3D usage) because it helps to imply detail in the model that does not exist in the geometry. (Image © Geoff Holman.)

4
The wheels on this tank are texture maps applied to much simpler geometry. Also notice that the turret and launchers are textured as one. (Image © Geoff Holman.)

4

PRODUCT VISUALIZATION

3D graphics also play an important role in product design. Prototypes and initial designs can be created and visualized entirely in the computer if necessary, and, though not a substitute for holding a real model, a 3D render makes presenting designs to a client a lot easier.

The beauty of 3D models, as opposed to real ones, is that they can be built once, but textured many times. Different material for a product can be visually tried out in minutes, and it's easy to change a part of a model without rebuilding the whole thing from scratch.

3

2

1

This minimal design shows how a 3D render can accurately represent the visual and textural qualities of a yet-to-be-built object. (Image © Dimitris Ladopoulos.)

2

Prototypes can be visualized using a variety of materials very simply. This simulation of computer hardware design by Dimitris Ladopoulos demonstrates how textures and materials can be convincingly conveyed using 3D graphics. (Image © Dimitris Ladopoulos.)

3

3D programs don't limit your arrangement of a product shot like gravity can. Creating images of products that do exist is another use for 3D rendering. It's often much cheaper to pay a single artist to render a product than to hire a photographer and studio. (Image © Dimitris Ladopoulos.)

4

Rendering an object from different angles and with dramatic lighting helps to gauge the form of an object from a single image. The stylish lines of this stool look very pleasing in this simple but effective render. (Image © Michael D. Abbott / Vantage Graphics & Design Ltd.)

4

182

GLOSSARY

3D Three dimensional; that is, an effect to give the illusion of depth on a flat page or monitor.

Aliasing The jagged edge of bitmapped images or fonts, occurring either when aliasing resolution is insufficient or when the images have been enlarged. This is caused by the pixels—which are square with straight sides—making up the image becoming visible. Sometimes called "jaggies," "staircasing," or "stairstepping."

Alpha channel A place where information regarding the transparency of a pixel is kept. In image files, this is a separate channel—additional to the three RGB or four CMYK channels—where "masks" are stored, simulating the physical material used in platemaking to shield parts of the plate from light.

Ambient A term used in 3D modeling software to describe a light source with no focus or direction, such as that which results from bouncing off all objects in a scene.

Animation (1) The process of creating a moving image by rapidly moving from one still image to the next. Traditionally, this was achieved through a laborious process of manually drawing or painting each "frame" (a single step in the animation) onto cellulose acetate sheets ("cels," or "cells"). However, animations are now more commonly created with specialized software that renders sequences in a variety of formats, typically QuickTime, AVI, Flash, and animated GIFs.

Animation (2) A "lossless" compression setting ("codec") used by QuickTime that will work with all bit depths. Since it is very sensitive to picture changes, the Animation codec works best for creating sequences in images that were rendered digitally.

Antialiasing A technique of optically eliminating the jagged effect of bitmapped images or text reproduced on low-resolution devices such as monitors. This is achieved by blending the color at the edges of the object with its background by averaging the density of the range of pixels involved. Antialiasing is also sometimes employed to filter texture maps, such as those used in 3D applications, to prevent moiré patterns.

API (Application Programing Interface) Special computer code supplied by a developer that can be used by other developers to implement a process in their software, such as OpenGL.

Area light A special light type that emits from a 2D area instead of a point.

Axis An imaginary line that defines the center of the 3D universe. In turn, the x, y, and z axes (width, height, and depth, respectively) define each of the three dimensions of an object. The axis along which an object rotates is the axis of rotation.

B-Spline A type of curve.

Bank Another term meaning to roll or rotate about an object's local z axis. Also applies when an object rotates along its motion vector.

Bevel To round or chamfer an edge. Can also mean to extrude a polygon along its Normal, producing bevels around its perimeter.

Bézier spline A Bézier curve in drawing applications is a curved line between two "control" points. Each point is a tiny database, or "vector," which stores information about the line, such as its thickness, color, length, and direction. Complex shapes can be applied to the curve by manipulating "handles," which are dragged out from the control points.

Bitmap Strictly speaking, any text character or image composed of dots. A bitmap is a "map" of "bits" which describes the complete collection of the bits that represent the location and binary state (on or off) of a corresponding set of items, such as pixels, which are required to form an image, as on a display monitor.

Blend The merging of two or more colors, forming a gradual transition from one to the other. Most graphics applications offer the facility for creating blends from any mix and any percentage of process colors. The quality of the blend is limited by the number of shades of a single color that can be reproduced without visible "banding." Since this limit is determined by the PostScript maximum of 256 levels, banding may become more visible when the values of a single color are very close (30 percent–60 percent, for example). However, blending two or more colors reduces the risk of banding.

Boolean Named after G. Boole, a 19th-century English mathematician, Boolean is used to describe a shorthand for logical computer operations, such as those that link values ("and," "or," "not," "nor," etc., called "Boolean operators"). For example, the search of a database could be refined using Boolean operators such as in "book and recent or new but not published." "Boolean expressions" compare two values and come up with the result ("return") of either "true" or "false," which are each represented by 1 and 0. In 3D applications, Boolean describes the joining or removing of one shape from another.

Bounding Box A rectangular box, available in certain applications, which encloses an item so that it can be resized or moved. In 3D applications, the bounding box is parallel to the axes of the object.

Buffer An area of computer memory set aside for the storage or processing of data while it is in transit. The buffer can be either in RAM or on a hard disk—within your computer, the buffer is called the "cache." Buffers are commonly used by output devices, such as modems and printers, which are then able to process data more quickly, while at the same time freeing up your computer so that you can keep on working.

Bump map A bitmap image file, normally grayscale, that is most frequently used in 3D applications for modifying surfaces or for applying textures. The gray values in the image are assigned height values, with black representing the troughs and white the peaks. Bump maps are used in the form of digital elevation models (DEMs) to generate cartographic relief maps.

CAD (computer-aided design) Strictly speaking, any design carried out using a computer, but the term is generally used with reference to 3D design, such as product design or architecture, where a computer software application is used to construct and develop complex structures.

Camera A device in which light passes through a lens to record an image. The image can be recorded onto presensitized film or paper, or by means of electronic sensors (CCDs) which digitally "write" the image to a storage device, such as a memory card or hard disk. In 3D, the camera is virtual and is used to define the rendered viewpoint. 3D cameras tend to have controls that mimic their real-world counterparts, such as zoom and field of view, lens type, shutter speed, etc.

Camera moves A feature of 3D applications that allows you to perform typical film and video camera movements in animated sequences, such as "pans," "tilts," "rolls," "dolly shots," and "tracking shots."

Cartesian coordinates A geometry system employed in 3D applications that uses numbers to locate a point on a plane in relation to an origin where one or more points intersect.

Channel Any animatable parameter. Can also mean one of the components of a material (for example, Diffuse channel).

Child An object linked hierarchically to another object (its "parent"). For example, if a "child" box is placed within—or linked to—a "parent" box, when the latter is moved, the child—and all its "grandchildren"!—move with it, retaining their relative positions and orientation. This enables manipulation of complex structures, particularly in 3D applications.

Clipping plane In 3D applications, a plane beyond which an object is not visible. A view of the world has six clipping planes: top, bottom, left, right, front, and back.

Collision detection The ability of a 3D program to calculate the proximity of objects and prevent them from intersecting.

Concave polygon A polygon whose shape is concave, for example, a star shape.

Convex polygon A polygon whose shape is convex, for example, a regular hexagon shape.

Coordinates Numerical values that define locations in 2D or 3D space.

Coplanar When points or polygons lie on the same plane.

Diffuse A material or surface property or channel. Diffuse shading is produced in the real world by subsurface scattering of light on an object. This process is simplified in 3D graphics, but the results are very similar.

Digital Anything operated by, or created from, information or signals represented by binary digits, such as a digital recording. As distinct from analog, in which information is represented by a physical variable (in a recording, this may be via the grooves in a vinyl platter).

Displacement map Offsetting the points of an object using the brightness values in an image.

Drop-off The effect of a value decreasing as the distance from a reference point increases. In lights the intensity may be set to drop off, the further from the light you get.

Environment map In 3D applications, a 2D image (PICT or BMP, for example) that is projected onto the surface of a 3D object to simulate an environmental reflection.

Exploded view An illustration of an object displaying its component parts separately—as though it were exploded—but arranged in such a way as to indicate their relationship within the whole object when assembled.

Extrapolate The term for creating new values for a parameter based on the values that have gone before.

Extrude The process of duplicating the cross-section of a 2D object, placing it in a 3D space at a distance from the original, and creating a surface that joins the two together. For example, two circles that become a tube.

Face Another name for a single polygon on a mesh.

Fall-off In a 3D environment, the degree to which light or any parameter loses intensity away from its source. (See also Drop-off.)

Field In documents and dialog boxes, the term generally describing any self-contained area into which data are entered. In video a field is a subframe that contains either every odd or every even line of pixels in an image.

Fillet (1) A curved surface that is created between two adjoining or intersecting surfaces (usually NURBS).

Fillet (2) A curved segment that joins two lines.

Forward Kinematics Traditional animation is based on Forward Kinematics, where, for example, to make a character reach for an object, first the upper arm is rotated, then the forearm, and then the hand.

Frame (1) An individual still image extracted from an animation sequence.

Frame (2) The name for the basic divisor of time in animation.

FPS (Frames Per Second) The number of individual still images that are required to make each second of an animation or movie sequence.

Frame rate Same as frames per second. The common frame rate for sequences used for computer display is 12–15 frames per second (fps), while in film it is 24fps, NTSC video 30fps, and PAL video 25fps.

Fresnel factor In a 3D environment, the brightening of the edge of an object by increasing the intensity of reflection along the edge, giving a more realistic visual effect.

Function curve A graphical representation of how an animated value changes over time. The function curve is a simple line in a graph that displays the value on one axis and time on the other.

Geometry What 3D objects are made out of, or rather described by. Geometry types include polygons, NURBS, and Bézier patches.

Gimbal lock In 3D applications, a situation in which an object cannot be rotated around one or more axes.

Glow A material parameter used to create external glows on objects. The glow usually extends beyond the object surface by a defined amount.

Gouraud shading A means by which 3D programs "fill in" the surface polygons of objects so that they look smooth and solid. The shading is derived by interpolating the surface vectors (called Normals) at each vertex to produce a graduated or smooth shaded look, as opposed to the faceted appearance that would result if no interpolation was done.

Grayscale The rendering of an image in a range of grays from white to black. In a digital image and on a monitor this usually means that an image is rendered with eight bits assigned to each pixel, giving a maximum of

256 levels of gray. Monochrome monitors (used increasingly rarely nowadays) can only display black pixels—in which case, grays are achieved by varying the number and positioning of black pixels using the technique called dithering.

Grid In some applications, a user-definable background pattern of equidistant vertical and horizontal lines to which elements such as guides, rules, type, boxes, etc., can be locked, or "snapped," thus providing greater positional accuracy.

Heading Local y-axis rotation. Part of the HPB rotation system (Heading Pitch Bank).

Height map An image used to displace or deform geometry. (See also Displacement.)

Hidden Surface Removal A rendering method, usually wire-frame, that prevents surfaces that cannot be seen from the given view from being drawn.

Hierarchy When objects are linked together to provide a priority system for certain operations. For example, a simple hierarchy might go, "upper leg > lower leg > foot." Moving the upper leg moves the lower leg and the foot by the same amount. If the foot is moved, the other two are not affected.

Interpolation A computer calculation used to estimate unknown values that fall between known ones. One use of this process is to redefine pixels in bitmapped images after they have been modified in some way, for instance, when an image is resized (called "resampling") or rotated, or if color corrections have been made. In such cases, the program makes estimates from the known values of other pixels lying in the same or similar ranges. Interpolation is also used by some scanning and image-manipulation software to enhance the resolution of images that have been scanned at low resolution. Inserting animation values between two keyframes of a sequence are also interpolations.

Inverse Kinematics Or IK for short. When animating hierarchical models, IK can be applied so that moving the lowest object in the hierarchy has an effect on all the objects further up. This is the inverse of how Forward Kinematics works.

Joint A special object type that does not render and can be used as the building blocks of skeletons, which in turn can be used to animate 3D models.

Kinematics Animated motion.

Lathe In 3D applications, the technique of creating a 3D object by rotating a 2D profile around an axis—just like carving a piece of wood on a real lathe.

Layer The grouping of objects into partitions so that they can easily be hidden or shown en masse.

Light The stuff that lets us see our 3D objects when we render our scene.

Magnet A tool that lets you pull and push the point on an object with a smooth drop-off effect.

Map Any image applied to a texture channel.

Mapping The process of applying textures to an object by defining a suitable projection method.

Material The aggregate of all surface attributes for an object.

Memory The recall of digital data on a computer. Typically, this refers to either "dynamic RAM," the volatile "random access" memory that is emptied when a computer is switched off (data need to be stored on media such as a hard disk for future renewal), or ROM, the stable "read only" memory that contains unchanging data, for example, the basic start-up and initialization functions of some computers, such as Macintosh. As an analogy, think of your own memory—when you die, everything in your head is lost unless you write it down, thus "saving" it for posterity. "Memory" is often erroneously used to describe "storage," probably because both are measured in megabytes.

Mesh Vertices that are linked together to form Polygon or NURBS (or other) surfaces.

Motion channel An animation parameter that controls how an object moves (for example, rotation x, y, z, and translation x, y, z are all Motion channels).

Move A tool used to translate 3D objects or components.

Multipass rendering The process whereby a single scene is rendered in multiple passes, each pass producing an image (or movie or image sequence) containing a specific portion of the scene but not all of it (for example, one part of a multipass render may contain just the reflections in the scene, or just the specular highlights. It may also contain single objects or effects).

Normal In 3D objects, the direction that is perpendicular to the surface of the polygon to which it relates.

Null A special object that has no geometry. Essentially it is an "empty" set of object axes. Nulls, however, are useful because objects can be linked to them, facilitating all manner of animation tricks. A camera may be linked to a hierarchy of Nulls for animation. The Nulls can be animated instead of the camera, preventing Gimbal lock (when a object cannot be rotated around one or more axes).

NURBS Non-Uniform Rational B-Spline. A special curve (and, when linked together, a surface) in 3D programs that is defined by a mathematical equation. Requires fewer points than polygons to achieve smooth flowing lines and surfaces.

Open (curve) A curve that does not form a closed loop.

Parallax The apparent movement of two objects relative to each other when viewed from different positions.

Parent In a hierarchy, the parent is the object to which a given object is linked below.

Phong shading Phong shading is a superior method of shading surfaces that computes the shading of every pixel by interpolating surface Normals.

Pitch The rotation around the x-axis as used in the HPB rotation system.

Pixel Acronym of picture element. The smallest component of a digitally generated image, such as a single dot of light on a computer monitor. In its simplest form, one pixel corresponds to a single bit: 0 = off, or white, and 1 = on, or black. In color or grayscale images or monitors, one pixel may correspond to several bits: an 8-bit pixel, for example, can be displayed in any of 256 colors (the total number of different configurations that can be achieved by eight 0s and 1s).

Plug-in Software, usually developed by a third party, that extends the capabilities of a particular program. Plug-ins are common in image-editing and page-layout applications for such things as special-effect filters. Plug-ins are also common in Web browsers for such things as playing movies and audio, although these often come as complete applications ("helper applications"), which can be used with a number of browsers rather than any specific one.

Polygon Composed of points joined by edges, polygons are the basic building blocks of 3D objects. They are not the only things that 3D objects can be constructed from, but when they are rendered, polygons are used 99 percent of the time.

Primitive The basic geometric element from which a complex object is built.

Quad A four-point polygon.

QuickTime Apple's software program and system extension that enables computers running either Windows or the Mac OS to play movie and sound files, particularly over the Internet and in multimedia applications, providing cut, copy, and paste features for moving images and automatic compression and decompression of image files.

RAM (**Random Access Memory**) A feature provided by some operating systems or utility software whereby a part of memory (RAM) can be temporarily "tricked" into thinking that that particular part is a disk drive. Because the process of retrieving data from RAM is so much faster than from disk, operations performed by items—such as applications or documents—stored in a RAM "disk" will speed up. This "disk" is erased when you switch your computer off.

Ray casting A no-bounce raytracing technique. (See Raytracing.)

Raytracing A rendering algorithm that simulates the physical and optical properties of light rays as they reflect off a 3D model, producing realistic shadows and reflections.

Real time The actual time in which things happen; on your computer, therefore, an event that corresponds to reality. For example, at its simplest, a character appearing on screen at the moment you type it is said to be real-time, as is a video sequence that plays back as it is being filmed. Also called "interactive mode."

Reflection The image of an environment or surrounding objects in the surface of a reflective object.

Refraction Light that is bent, typically when passing through one medium to another, such as air to water.

Rendering The process of creating a 2D image from 3D geometry to which lighting effects and surface textures have been applied.

RGB Red, green, blue. The primary colors of the "additive" color model—used in video technology (including computer monitors) and for graphics (for the Web and multimedia, for example) that will not ultimately be printed by the four-color (CMYK) process method.

Roll In a 3D environment, the rotation of an object or camera around the z-axis.

Rotate A 3D transformation that turns an object about one or more axes.

Round To bevel an edge or vertex.

Scale A 3D transformation that shrinks or enlarges an object about one or more axes.

Shading The process of filling in the polygons of a 3D model with respect to viewing angle and lighting conditions.

Skin In 3D applications, a surface stretched over a series of "ribs," such as an aircraft wing.

Snapping In many applications, a facility which automatically guides the positioning of items along invisible grid lines, objects, components, etc., aiding design and layout.

Specular map In 3D applications, a texture map—such as those created by noise filters—that is used instead of specular color to control highlights.

Spline The digital representation of a curved line that is defined by three or more control points.

Stitching A technique in NURBS modeling whereby two or more surfaces are joined along their boundaries.

Storyboard A sequence of drawings used to lay out the action and camera angles in a film or animation.

Surface In 3D applications, the matrix of control points and line end points underlying a mapped texture or color.

Surface geometry In 3D applications, the geometry that underlies a surface, becoming visible when the surface is simplified.

Sweep The process of creating a 3D object by moving a profile along a path.

Texture The surface definition of an object.

Texture filtering A method for improving (or reducing) the quality of textures for use in 3D programs.

Tiling An image repeated two or more times to create a background. A background image, smaller than the size of the screen (which is, in turn, arbitrary), is automatically tiled to fill the screen.

Transformation tool In some applications, the name given to tools that change the location or appearance of an item, such as scale, rotate, and move.

Triangle The simplest type of polygon is a triangle that is made from three connected vertices.

UV coordinates In a 3D environment, a system of rectangular 2D coordinates used to apply a texture map to a 3D surface.

Vertex Another name for a point (polygons) or control point (NURBS).

View A window in a 3D program depicting the 3D scene from a given vantage.

Wire-frame A skeletal view, or a computer-generated 3D object before the surface rendering has been applied.

Z-Buffer A 3D renderer that solves the problem of rendering two pixels in the same place (one in front of the other) by calculating and storing the distance of each pixel from the camera (the "z-distance"), then rendering the nearest pixel last.

187

INDEX

189

ACKNOWLEDGMENTS

Picture credits

AKG, LONDON
10 top: Santa Maria della Grazie Refectory, Milan; 11 top: AKG, LONDON/Erich Lessing.

BRIDGEMAN ART LIBRARY, LONDON
10 center: Scrovegni (Arena) Chapel, Padua; 11 bottom: Birmingham Museum and Art Gallery; 11 right: Metropolitan Museum of Art, New York.

CORBIS
32–33: Toshiyuki Aizanwa/Reuters NewMedia Inc.; 87 bottom: Paul A. Souders; 128: Hulton-Deutsch Coll.; 129: Duomo.

THE KOBAL COLLECTION, LONDON
32 bottom: Disney/Pixar © Disney Enterprises Inc.; 33: Paramount; 36–37 and 37: Ben Jade/Large-Pringle/Allied Vision; 87 bottom: © Warner Bros.

THE SCIENCE PHOTO LIBRARY:
36–37 top: NASA.

Copyright Notice